# RHODE ISLAND
### AND THE
# CIVIL WAR

# RHODE ISLAND
## AND THE
# CIVIL WAR

*Voices from the Ocean State*

ROBERT GRANDCHAMP
FOREWORD BY FRANK J. WILLIAMS

Charleston · London
THE
History
PRESS

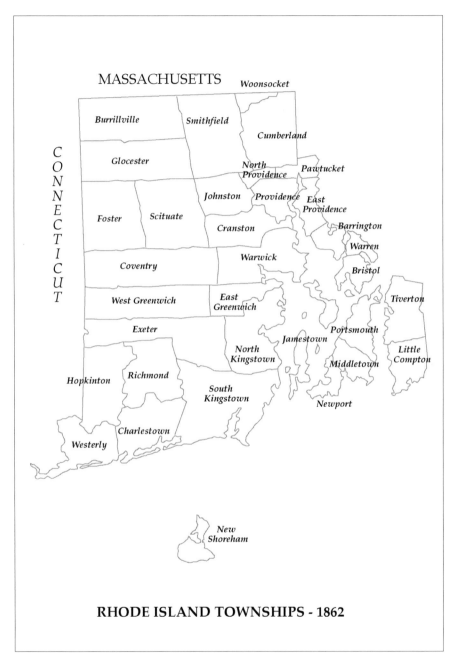

MASSACHUSETTS

Woonsocket

Burrillville

Smithfield

Cumberland

C
O
N
N
E
C
T
I
C
U
T

Glocester

North
Providence

Pawtucket

Johnston

Providence

East
Providence

Foster

Scituate

Cranston

Barrington

Warren

Coventry

Warwick

Bristol

West Greenwich

East
Greenwich

Tiverton

Exeter

Jamestown

Portsmouth

North
Kingstown

Middletown

Little
Compton

Hopkinton

Richmond

South
Kingstown

Newport

Charlestown

Westerly

New
Shoreham

**RHODE ISLAND TOWNSHIPS - 1862**

Rhode Island in the 1860s.

Published by The History Press
Charleston, SC 29403
www.historypress.net

Copyright © 2012 by Robert Grandchamp
All rights reserved

All images are from the collection of author Robert Grandchamp.

First published 2012

Manufactured in the United States

ISBN 978.1.60949.761.3

Library of Congress CIP data applied for.

*To Kris VanDenBossche and Ken Carlson.*
*For laying a steady foundation on which others will follow.*

# Contents

# Foreword

S omething like sixty-five thousand books have been published on the Civil War, more than one a day since it ended. But between the study and the storytelling, there is a tremendous lack of consensus about what the Civil War means.

Robert Grandchamp's *Rhode Island and the Civil War: Voices from the Ocean State* is the tonic that all Rhode Islanders and students of the American Civil War need during our sesquicentennial of this great and horrific conflict. In 1964, General Harold R. Barker wrote and published the *History of the Rhode Island Combat Units in the Civil War (1861–1865)*. Robert Grandchamp's study is a much-needed update of that seminal work.

Rhode Island, like every state in America, keenly felt the impact of the Civil War. Many Rhode Islanders hoped to avoid this conflict. Those producing cotton textiles—and there were many in Rhode Island—had economic ties with the South, relationships that war would end.

When the Rhode Island Republican Party nominated Seth Padelford (whose antislavery views were extreme) for governor in 1860, a split occurred in the party ranks. Republican moderates and supporters of Abraham Lincoln joined with Democrats (who were soft on slavery) to nominate and elect a fusion candidate on a "Conservative" ticket. William Sprague of Cranston, the thirty-year-old heir to a vast cotton textile empire and a military man who had attained the rank of colonel in the Providence Marine Corps of Artillery, was the choice. He outpolled Padelford 12,278 to 10,740, a rebuff to abolitionism.

Yet the Rhode Island citizenry was still strong for the Union. After the Confederate attack on Fort Sumter on April 12, 1861, Rhode Islanders rallied behind the governor. President Lincoln issued his first call for 75,000 volunteers on April 15. Just three days later, the "Flying Artillery"—a battery of light artillery of the Providence Marine Corps of Artillery on Benefit Street, Providence—left for the front, and on April 20, Colonel Ambrose Burnside and Sprague himself led 530 men of the First Regiment, Rhode Island Detached Militia, from Exchange Place to their first fateful encounter with the Rebels at Bull Run.

There were eight calls for troops during the war, and as the author points out, Rhode Island exceeded its requisition in all but one. While the state's total quota was 18,898, it furnished 23,236 fighting men, proportionately more than any other state in the Union—even though the draft was required from time to time. About 2,000 died of wounds or disease, and more than 20 earned the Medal of Honor. Despite its small size, Rhode Island played an important role in the Civil War by sending eight infantry regiments, four artillery regiments and three cavalry regiments with several smaller units. Rhode Island troops fought in every major engagement of the war from Bull Run to Antietam, Fredericksburg, Gettysburg and Appomattox. The Fourteenth Rhode Island Heavy Artillery (Colored) did not see combat but served honorably under difficult conditions in Texas and New Orleans. Two famous generals, Ambrose Burnside and George Sears Greene, were from Rhode Island and served nobly, despite the controversy still surrounding the former over the defeat of his Army of the Potomac at Fredericksburg.

In 1862, Fort Adams in Newport became the headquarters and recruit depot for the Fifteenth U.S. Infantry Regiment, and the USS *Rhode Island*, a side-wheel steamer, was commissioned in 1861 for the Union navy. It intercepted blockade-runners in the West Indies and later was a part of the South Atlantic Blockading Squadron.

During the conflict, Melville in Portsmouth became the site of a military hospital, while Newport became the home of the United States Naval Academy during the war, relocated from Annapolis, as it was so close to the combat zone. The Academy occupied a hotel known as Atlantic House at the corner of Bellevue Avenue and Pelham Street, with training ships and instructional facilities on Goat Island.

The state's contribution to the Union victory went beyond mere military and naval manpower. The productive capacity of Northern industry was a decisive element in the outcome of the Civil War, and Rhode Island was a prominent contributor. Its woolen mills supplied Federal troops, including Rhode Islanders, with thousands of uniforms, overcoats and blankets, while metal factories provided guns, sabers and musket parts. The Builders Iron Foundry, operating in Warwick, manufactured a large number of cannons, and the Providence Steam Engine Company built the engines for two Union sloops of war, with Congdon & Carpenter supplying the military with hardware. While Robert Grandchamp's book covers military engagements and Rhode Island's participation, we must not forget the homefront and its significant contribution to Union victory.

The author focuses on Rhode Island units, and he presents more than an introductory review into Rhode Island's war effort. His brief but detailed narrative of each unit is based on letters, diaries and regimental histories, providing a new source of information for Rhode Islanders to learn about the Civil War. This he does in exquisite fashion.

The author also provides a short but helpful bibliography, as well as the names of the Rhode Island "boys" who earned the Medal of Honor.

We cannot come to terms with the Civil War because it presents us with an unacceptable kind of self-knowledge. We think, as Americans, that we possess a heroic past, and we like to think of our history as one of progress and the spread of freedom. But the Civil War tells us that we possess a tragic history instead, over which we must continually hope. Words from the war convey a bracing candor and individuality, traits Americans reflexively extoll while rarely exhibiting. But in this book, you can hear the bold voices in the writing of common soldiers, their letters untouched by military censors and their dialect not yet homogenized by television.

During the next four years, the Rhode Island Civil War Sesquicentennial Commemoration Commission will attempt to refresh our memory of those days at home and in the field, with the hope that our divided state will reconcile and each of us will be more civil.

It is a bottomless treasure, the Civil War, much of it encrusted in myth or still unexplored. Which is why, a century and a half later, it stills claims our attention.

Frank J. Williams
Chair, Rhode Island Civil War
Sesquicentennial Commemoration Commission
Hope Valley, Rhode Island
June 6, 2012

# Foreword

*Frank J. Williams is a retired chief justice of the Rhode Island Supreme Court and one of the country's most renowned experts on Abraham Lincoln. He is the author or editor of more than fourteen books. At the same time, he has amassed an unsurpassed private library and archive that ranks among the nation's largest and finest Lincoln collections. In 2000, the chief justice was appointed to the United States Abraham Lincoln Bicentennial Commission created by Congress to plan events to commemorate the 200th birthday of Abraham Lincoln in 2009. He also served as a captain in the U.S. Army during Vietnam, earning the Bronze Star and Air Medal. He served as chief judge of the U.S. Court of Military Commission Review from November 21, 2007, to December 23, 2009.*

# Acknowledgements

I spent nearly ten years of my life living in Rhode Island studying the Civil War and its continued impact on my home state. Traveling every corner of Rhode Island, from Little Compton to Burrillville, and many places in between, I met hundreds of individuals who graciously shared their time, energy and resources to help me in my many projects over the years. Although I am no longer a resident of the state, many of them continue to assist me to this day. In no particular order, they include Kris VanDenBossche, Mike Lannigan, Phil DiMaria, General Richard Valente, Rachel Peirce, Midge Frazel, Ken Carlson, Frank Williams, Nina Wright, Edna Kent, Mark Dunkelman, Tom Keenan, Jim Crothers, Scott Bill Hirst, Matt Reardon, Shirley Arnold, Fred Faria, Peg Pinkey, Betty Mancucci, CSM Thomas Caruolo, Leo Kennedy, Stanley Lemons, Ron Dufour, Elisa Miller, George Matteson, Ivy Brunelle, Marlene Lopes, Frank Gryzb, Rick Ring and Craig Anthony.

In addition, thanks go to the staffs at the following repositories: Langworthy Library; Westerly Public Library; Providence Public Library; Rhode Island Historical Society; Providence Marine Corps of Artillery; Richmond Historical Society; Pettaquamscutt Historical Society; Newport Historical Society; Rhode Island Civil War Round Table; New England Civil War Museum; Glocester Heritage Society; Burrillvillle Historical Society; Rhode Island Sons of Union Veterans; Battery B, First Rhode Island Light Artillery; South County Museum; Scituate Preservation Society; Greene Public Library; Warwick Historical Society;

## Acknowledgements

Foster Preservation Society; Tyler Free Library; North Kingstown Public Library; and the Western Rhode Island Civic Historical Society.

To those not mentioned above, thank you for the assistance in remembering Rhode Island's Boys in Blue.

# Introduction

From Adamsville, Quonochontaug, Usquepaugh, Lime Rock, Rockville and Rice City, they answered the call. From Westerly in the south to Cumberland in the north, they came. Between 1861 and 1865, more than twenty-three thousand men from Rhode Island responded to the call to arms from President Abraham Lincoln to save "the last best hope for mankind." They marched into combat under a blue flag emblazoned with the fowled anchor of their state, bearing the motto "In Te Domine Speramus" ("Our Hope Is in Thee Lord"). Men from the smallest state served in eight infantry regiments, ten batteries of light artillery, three regiments of heavy artillery, and three regiments and a battalion of cavalry, as well as in the Regular Army, Marine Corps and U.S. Navy. Rhode Islanders left a record unsurpassed in the conflict for such a small state. Fighting in nearly every major engagement of the war—from the famous battles of Antietam, Spotsylvania and Gettysburg to more obscure actions such as Pocotaligo, Red River and Bethesda Church—Rhode Island soldiers made their marks on the battlefield and off. After four years of bloody conflict, the nation was preserved and slavery destroyed, and more than two thousand men from Rhode Island were dead.

While most people in their late teens and early twenties went to clubs in Providence and other local dives, I was different. My spare time was spent in Providence as well, but at the Rhode Island Historical Society, Brown University and the Rhode Island State Archives. When others shunned graveyards as unpleasant places to visit, I took the time to visit each Civil

War-era cemetery in Rhode Island, searching every corner of my home state for its forgotten Civil War heroes "whose bodies now lie in almost every city, village, and hamlet churchyard in the land." Today, earth covers the graves of more than twenty-three thousand of these men, but each marker, each man, has a story to tell. Visiting these graveyards and seeking out the letters preserved has allowed a window to the past to open, one that illustrates as clearly as can be permitted life a century and a half ago.

During the six years I spent as a student at Rhode Island College, eventually earning an MA in American history, I collected boxes of material relating to Rhode Island in the Civil War era. Traveling to each archive, library and repository in the state, painstakingly reading Civil War-era newspapers and reaching out to scores of descendants, I gathered enough material over the years to write several in-depth books on Rhode Island in the period. These volumes are history-heavy, fact-based narratives about particular Rhode Island units. Today, the material used to write these books is housed at the University of Rhode Island and Rhode Island College Special Collections for future researchers to use. Moving to Vermont has refocused my research, but I continue to seek new information on the boys from Rhode Island.

This book is a departure from my normal tone of historical writing. Rather, *Rhode Island and the Civil War: Voices from the Ocean State* is designed to serve as an introductory volume to Rhode Island in the Civil War era. Designed for those with an interest but who do not wish to obtain a scholarly standing, this book will introduce each unit fielded by Rhode Island in the War of the Rebellion, when and how they were raised, where they fought and what happened to them. Each regimental summary is highlighted by quotes from soldiers who served in the unit, while photographs, many never before published, connect the reader to these brave soldiers. Furthermore, the official battle honors, the same names inscribed on the flags at the Rhode Island Statehouse, are given as well. As this is an introductory text, notes are only used in the portion related to the Peckham letters in an appendix, but the "Further Reading" chapter will present books for those wanting to learn more.

Although many books have been written by and about Rhode Island's role in the Civil War over the years, this book is for the people of the Ocean State to learn more about those men from Little Rhody who served, fought and died to save the Union 150 years ago.

# Chapter 1

# Rhode Island Responds

The storm burst on April 12, 1861, when Confederate troops opened fire on Federal-occupied Fort Sumter in Charleston Harbor, South Carolina. Three days later, President Abraham Lincoln issued a call for seventy-five thousand volunteers to suppress the rebellion in the South. Governor William Sprague, the "boy governor" at only thirty-one, was the scion of a wealthy Cranston textile family. Elected the year before, he had spent thousands of dollars of his own money reequipping and preparing the Rhode Island Militia for war. When the president called for men, Sprague promised that Rhode Island would do its "utmost" to preserve the Union.

The same night that he received the call for volunteers, Sprague sent a message to a down-on-his-luck railroad executive in New York City. A West Pointer, this man had been stationed at Fort Adams in Newport before he was resigned to open a rifle factory in Bristol. Although innovative at the time, no one bought the breech-loader in the quantities needed to make a profit. When his creditors moved in, this former soldier sold his business and became a cashier at the Illinois Central Railroad under his old friend George B. McClellan. In his April 15 telegraph, Sprague wrote that a Rhode Island regiment was being raised immediately for field service and asked this former soldier if he wanted to command the unit—and, if so, when he could arrive in Providence. Elated by the news, this man replied, "Immediately." Ambrose Everett Burnside became the first man to officially volunteer for duty from the state of Rhode Island and Providence Plantations.

Governor William Sprague led the
men of his state to war in 1861.

Rhode Islanders were no strangers to war. From the beginning, settlers
had contended that a well-regulated militia was a necessity for the common
defense. In 1675, King Philip's War erupted throughout much of Rhode
Island as colonists and natives battled over control of the land. Throughout
the colonial wars of the first half of the eighteenth century, Rhode Islanders
fought side by side with British regulars in Canada, New York and the
Caribbean. In 1775, the Rhode Island Militia went to war to establish a
government of its own, sending three regiments to join the Continental
army, men who fought with Washington in nearly every major battle of the
war. At home, the militiamen watched as war came to their footsteps, with
the British capture of Newport in 1776 and the eventual Battle of Rhode
Island in 1778. With British raids into the interior a constant threat, the
militia spent nearly eight years guarding the state's vast four-hundred-mile
coastline. During the War of 1812, Rhode Islanders again responded, as
they did in 1846, sending one company to fight in Mexico with the New
England Volunteers.

While other states in the Jacksonian era abolished their state militias,
Rhode Island embraced the idea of elite volunteer companies, men who
paid dues to belong to organizations, bought their own uniforms and took
pride in belonging to such exotic corps as the Providence Marine Corps of

The Rhode Island Militia was ready to take the field in 1861. Pictured here in his Kentish Guards uniform is Samuel E. Rice of East Greenwich. As a sergeant in Company H, Seventh Rhode Island, he died at Spotsylvania.

Artillery, Westerly Rifles, Kentish Guards and First Light Infantry. Meeting weekly in their armories, they excelled in military drill and discipline; state officers from neighboring Massachusetts and Connecticut frequently visited Providence to learn the latest tactics. Although the militias of the time are often portrayed as little more than social clubs, the units from Rhode Island trained hard. In 1842, when Rhode Island nearly erupted in civil war during the Dorr Rebellion, the militia quickly responded, preventing an infusion of blood, during engagements in Providence, Chepachet and Pawtucket. Throughout the 1850s, the chartered companies perfected their organization, training a valuable cadre of officers to take command when the call came. It was obvious to many that the United States could no longer endure being half slave and half free.

The Rhode Island economy depended on Southern cotton to keep the many mills in the state open. Despite this, and the resulting economic downturn, the factories quickly retooled for war. Cotton factories in Ashland, Carolina and Rockland began making blankets and the coarse wool for Federal blue uniforms. In Forrestdale, the local scythe works started making swords, while in Bristol and Providence, the Providence Tool Company and the Burnside Rifle Company produced thousands of arms for the cause. At home, mothers, wives, daughters and sweethearts sent thousands of care

*Left*: Major General Ambrose E. Burnside was the first Rhode Islander to volunteer his services and became the most famous soldier from the state.

*Below*: The Burnside Expedition, which contained members of the Fourth and Fifth Rhode Island and Battery F, landed in North Carolina in 1862.

The rural mill village of Ashland in southern Scituate was typical of the communities from which Rhode Island soldiers came.

packages to the front to support the men in the field. From the start, Rhode Island devoted itself to the cause of preserving the Union.

Perhaps it was the noble sense of freeing the slave or perhaps the chance to leave the factory or farm to find adventure or taste glory on the battlefield, but when the call was issued that April day, it was instantly responded to by men from across Rhode Island. First to respond was the Providence Marine Corps of Artillery, a battery of light artillery in Providence. Two days before the firing on Sumter, Sprague wrote to the president, "We have a Battery of Light Artillery, 6 pdrs, horses + men complete—Unsurpassed or at any rate not surpassed by a similar number in any country—who would respond at short notice to the call of the government for the defence of the capital. The artillery especially, I imagine would be very serviceable." Leaving Providence on the morning of April 18, 1861, the battery later claimed to be the first organized group of men to respond to the president's call. Stopping briefly in Pennsylvania, they exchanged their old smoothbore guns for James rifles, becoming the first unit in the United States Army to be armed with rifled cannons.

Two days later, the First Rhode Island Detached Militia, an infantry regiment under the command of Colonel Burnside, left for Washington. Chaplain Augustus Woodbury remembered what he felt when he went to war:

Despite his losing a leg at Fredericksburg, William and Lucretia Rathbun maintained a farm in Coventry.

# Rhode Island Responds

*It seemed as though almost the entire population of the State of Rhode Island crowded the streets of Providence to witness the departure of this gallant band of soldiers, and to bid them God-speed upon their dangerous enterprise. The wharves, the heights upon the shores of the harbor, and the coasts of Narragansett Bay, were crowded with spectators. Cannon belched forth its thunder. Cheers of men rent the air. The prayers and blessings of tearful women consecrated the hour. As the steamer, in which the command had embarked, left the bay, and entered upon the waters beyond, the boom of the heavy Columbiads upon the parapet of Fort Adams announced to those upon the sea and those upon the land, that the shores of Rhode Island had been left, perhaps forever, by the flower of her youth and the prime of her manhood.*

Arriving in Washington, the Rhode Island troops organized Camp Sprague as a training camp. In May, the governor again issued a call, this time raising another regiment, the Second Rhode Island, and another battery. Quickly raised, the Second joined the First at Camp Sprague preparing to go to the front. On July 21, 1861, Colonel Burnside received his chance. Eager for action, President Lincoln urged an attack. It came at a place called Bull Run. Burnside's men led the assault that morning, firing the first shots of the battle at a place called Matthew's Hill. For forty-five minutes, the Second Rhode Island held off constant Confederate attacks. Colonel John Stanton Slocum, a native of Richmond, fell mortally wounded as he cheered his men with the words, "Now show them what Rhode Island can do!" These words became a rallying call for Rhode Islanders for the next four years. With the help of the First Rhode Island, the Confederates were pushed back, but not without heavy losses for the Rhode Island units. Retreating to Washington, the First Rhode Island, a three-month regiment, was mustered out. More than 60 percent of the men reenlisted, providing a solid backbone of proven combat leadership in every Rhode Island regiment. The Second Rhode Island remained at Camp Sprague, eventually becoming one of the most famous infantry regiments in the Army of the Potomac.

With the defeat at Bull Run, Sprague again issued calls for Rhode Island troops. By the end of 1861, the Third, Fourth and Fifth Regiments of infantry were on their way to locations in North and South Carolina. Meanwhile, veterans of the Providence Marine Corps of Artillery stayed behind at their arsenal on Benefit Street, helping to drill and recruit men for the light batteries. Eventually, eight batteries joined the First Rhode Island Light Artillery Regiment. The First Rhode Island Cavalry was also raised in

*Above*: A veteran of the Mexican-American War, Colonel John Stanton Slocum of the Second Rhode Island was killed at Bull Run.

*Right*: Samuel J. English rose from private to captain in the Second Rhode Island.

# Rhode Island Responds

General Augustus Mauran served as adjutant general during the Civil War.

December 1861, recruiting its men from throughout the state, and included a battalion of New Hampshire troops. At Fort Adams, in Newport, Regular Army recruiters joined in the process, eventually recruiting nearly one thousand men for the professional service. Although there was opportunity to work in the mills and the gun factories were booming with orders for goods, many Rhode Island men took a reduction in pay to join the service. Schoolteachers who were earning $50 a month, plus room and board, joined up as privates, earning $13 a month. Although the state bounty was only $100, the units quickly filled. In May 1861, Charles Slade Nichols of Hopkinton had offered his silver watch and $50 for a spot in the Second Rhode Island; now he got the coveted spot without paying the money.

In the winter of 1862, Ambrose Burnside, now a brigadier general, raised a division of troops from the New England states that included Battery F, First Rhode Island Light Artillery, as well as the Fourth and Fifth Rhode Island. Launching an amphibious assault off the coast of North Carolina, the troops captured the seacoast of the state, with the Fourth Rhode Island leading a decisive charge at the Battle of New Berne. In April, the Third

*Left*: The arsenal of the
Providence Marine Corps of
Artillery on Benefit Street was the
departure point for many Rhode
Islanders on their way to war.

*Below*: The Providence Marine
Corps of Artillery claimed to be
the first unit of Northern militia
to respond to Lincoln's call of
April 1861.

Rhode Island, which was now a heavy artillery regiment, used its long-range cannons to compel Fort Pulaski to surrender in Savannah, Georgia. In the Shenandoah Valley, the First Rhode Island Cavalry saw constant action in small skirmishes, while on the Virginia Peninsula, the Second Rhode Island and five batteries of artillery followed George McClellan's army in every movement, fighting at Fair Oaks and the Seven Days Battles.

In the late summer of 1862, Rhode Island troops again fought with their usual ardor, seeing combat at Cedar Mountain, Groveton, Second Bull Run and Chantilly. On September 17, at Antietam, the bloodiest day in American history, units from Rhode Island quite literally opened the battle and ended it as well. Fighting the Rebels in cornfields, woodlots and farmer's fields, the soldiers of Batteries A, D and G, as well as the Fourth Rhode Island, lost heavily at Dunker Church, Bloody Lane and Otto's Farm, but their sacrifice allowed Abraham Lincoln to make the war a moral crusade by issuing the Emancipation Proclamation. At home, another infantry regiment, the Seventh, in addition to a cavalry unit, a battalion of heavy artillery and another battery were also mustered in the fall of 1862. Furthermore, two regiments, the Eleventh and the Twelfth, recruited for a nine-month deployment.

The darkest day for Rhode Island in the Civil War was December 13, 1862. General Burnside, now in command of the Army of the Potomac, had to attack the Confederates to attempt to end the war by the end of the year, when the Emancipation Proclamation would go into effect. Pressured from Washington, he ordered his men forward against the city of Fredericksburg, Virginia. This battle represented the largest gathering of Rhode Island troops in one place during the entire war. The smallest state was represented on the field by the Second, Fourth, Seventh and Twelfth Rhode Island Infantry Regiments, the First Rhode Island Cavalry and Batteries A, B, C, D, E and G of the First Rhode Island Light Artillery. Burnside's orders were misinterpreted as thousands of Union troops marched to their deaths below a hill known as Marye's Heights. The Twelfth Rhode Island, a new regiment, disintegrated under fire, while the Seventh continued to push forward, losing men for every yard it advanced. Battery B distinguished itself by going into action close to the Confederate line to support the infantry. Drummer William P. Hopkins of West Greenwich later recalled, "Barrels of blood had been poured on the ground." It was the bloodiest single day in Rhode Island history. When the sun set that December day, seventy-five Rhode Islanders were dead and more than three hundred more wounded; eleven of the dead came from South Kingstown. Tryphena Cundall was a devout Seventh Day

Francis Adams of Providence served in the U.S. Navy.

Baptist from Hopkinton who kept a journal during the war. She also had a son, Isaac, who was a member of the Seventh Rhode Island. When the news of Fredericksburg was received at home in Ashaway, she wrote:

> *It is reported our loss is 13,000 killed, wounded, or missing. What a multitude to be swept off at once, many thousands wounded. Oh the anguish, the pain with no wife or mother or sister to sooth or nurse or even to give a cup of water. My heart aches for the loved ones many very many have fallen to rise no more but to be huddled into the grave of a battlefield.*

# Rhode Island Responds

*Many more will die of wounds received on the 13th of December 1862 at Fredericksburg Virginia and many more will linger out a life maimed crippled and suffering. What can I write, how can I express my feelings, it is in vain to try.*

Burnside accepted blame for the defeat and was transferred to a command in the West.

After Fredericksburg, the soldiers from Rhode Island did their best to cope with the loss of so many friends and comrades while trying to survive a bleak winter in Virginia. To help the men from his state, Governor Sprague, soon to be appointed to the U.S. Senate and replaced with James Y. Smith, appointed Charlotte Dailey and several Rhode Island doctors to visit the camps in Virginia. Mrs. Dailey found hundreds of Rhode Islanders suffering from lack of proper food, clothing and shoes. To combat the problem, citizens from Newport chartered two ships to bring relief to the soldiers in the state. Meanwhile, the state had established a large hospital at Portsmouth Grove the previous summer, allowing troops not just from Rhode Island but also from elsewhere a place to recover away from the war zone.

Rhode Island troops were actively engaged at Chancellorsville, where the Second Rhode Island took an active role at the Battle of Salem's Church, while Batteries A, E and G distinguished themselves as well. The small community of Scituate lost nine of its sons in the battle. Two months later, Rhode Island troops again distinguished themselves at Gettysburg, with three batteries being in the center of the storm, and the Second Rhode Island completing an epic forty-mile march to get to the battlefield.

By the summer of 1863, Rhode Islanders could be justly proud of their contribution to the Union cause. By this point, the state had raised all of its units. The Fourteenth Rhode Island Heavy Artillery, a black regiment, went to garrison a series of forts near New Orleans, while the Third Rhode Island Cavalry fought guerillas in Louisiana as well. In Mississippi, the Seventh Rhode Island fought at Vicksburg, while Battery D was stationed in Kentucky. In South Carolina, the Third Rhode Island Heavy Artillery was actively engaged in siege operations against Fort Wagner and Fort Sumter. In North Carolina, the Fifth Rhode Island held a series of forts on the North Carolina coast, while the Fourth Rhode Island picketed near Suffolk, Virginia. The First Rhode Island Cavalry actively fought the Rebels in northern Virginia, while the Second Rhode Island and five batteries of artillery ably served with the Army of the Potomac.

In levels of high command, Rhode Islanders were no strangers either. Frank Wheaton led a division in the Sixth Corps, while Warwick's George Sears Greene, at sixty one of the oldest field commanders in the army, led a brigade in the Twelfth Corps. In Washington, Major General Silas Casey had written the army's main infantry tactics manual and now led the board that appointed officers to the United States Colored Troops. In the Department of the Gulf, Richard Arnold of Providence and Thomas West Sherman of Newport both held important commands. General Burnside led an advance into east Tennessee and then was retransferred east with his Ninth Corps. It is hard to imagine that all of these contributions came from a state barely forty-five miles long and thirty-five miles wide.

By the spring of 1864, Rhode Islanders were long used to the cost of war; few did not know of a friend, neighbor or family member who had died in the service. The Overland Campaign, fought in the spring of 1864, brought increased losses to the state. For forty days, the men from Rhode Island were constantly engaged in a death struggle with the Confederacy. The *Providence Journal* carried casualty lists from places many had never heard of: the Wilderness, Spotsylvania Court House, Po River, Totopotomoy, North Anna, Cold Harbor and Petersburg. In a moving letter to the adjutant general of Rhode Island, Lieutenant Colonel Percy Daniels of the Seventh Rhode Island attempted to explain what happened to his regiment:

> *Look on the bloodstained hills, in the desolate valleys, and among the battle-scarred forests from the Rapidan to the Appomattox, and you can see where many of them sleep, and though their places are vacant their names are sacred and encircled with a halo of glory. Many others have returned to their friends maimed with deformities they must carry to the grave, but they, while here, will be cared for and loved, and when they pass away their names shall be remembered. Hard indeed has been the work and terrible the carnage of the past two months, and not soon shall we forget the 10th, 11th, 12th, 13th, and 18th of May, when we shared in the hard struggle around Spotsylvania, nor the fighting of the 24th, 25th, and 26th across the North Anna. The skirmishers of the 30th and 31st of May and 1st and 2nd of June at Totopotomoy Creek will, too, be remembered, and the bloody charge of the 3rd of June, when one-third of the regiment went down, will never be forgotten. Our hard marches also, which have not been few, have left their impression, as well as the many nights we have used the shovel and pick in the trenches and pits. But through all the Seventh has shown a gallantry, coolness, fidelity, and perseverance worthy her native*

# Rhode Island Responds

*State, and we hope no Rhode Islander can look on our record with any but the feelings of pride, though his joy must be tinged with sadness for the fallen brave. They have added much to the bright laurels won in previous campaigns, and nobly earned a soldier's brightest reward—the approbation of his superiors. Our decimated ranks tell of the hard work we have done. You would hardly recognize our short line of to-day as all that is left of the 900 that left Rhode Island with us less than two years ago; but though the chances of war have called us to weep over the graves of so many noble comrades, those that remain are true as steel, as has been proven on many a hard-fought field. May the future be as free from dishonor as the past.*

Rhode Island troops in the field continued to persevere as those at home waited for the war to end.

In the fall of 1864, Rhode Islanders again fought hard at Poplar Spring Church, while in the Shenandoah Valley, the Second Rhode Island Volunteers, First Rhode Island Cavalry and Batteries C, D and G formed an important part of the Union force that defeated the Confederates at Opequon, Fisher's Hill and Cedar Creek. In November, the men in the field and those at home again overwhelmingly supported President Lincoln in his reelection. By April 2, 1865, soldiers from the Second Rhode Island and Battery G were among the first to storm into Petersburg, thus breaking the Confederate line. A week later, Robert E. Lee surrendered at Appomattox, nearly four years to the day after Lincoln had called Rhode Island to send its sons to war. To celebrate the victory, the Seventh Rhode Island, which included several Narragansett Indians, organized "a grand powwow over it," celebrating well into the night. After expending so much treasure and blood, the conflict was finally over.

From June until December 1865, the Rhode Island troops slowly returned home. Always greeting them at Fox Point at Providence was a victory salute fired by the Providence Marine Corps of Artillery, a parade of state militia, a hearty meal and a "welcome home" speech by the governor. Many returned home to pick up their shattered lives, never forgetting the horrific sights they had witnessed, while returning to work in the shops, mills and farms they left behind. Many veterans took great pride in their war service, literally taking it to the grave with an inscription on their headstone that they had served in the Rhode Island Volunteers.

The pages that follow have brief summaries of the contributions that each Rhode Island regiment gave to the war.

# Chapter 2

# The Infantry

## FIRST RHODE ISLAND DETACHED MILITIA

When the call to arms came in April 1861, the Rhode Island Militia was perhaps the most disciplined, ready-to-respond force in New England behind that of Massachusetts. Within five days of the recruiting call, 1,100 men were raised, uniformed, armed and on their way to the front in two detachments under Colonel Burnside, while Governor Sprague, exercising his right as "captain-general" of the state militia, personally accompanied the unit. The ten companies of the First were drawn exclusively from the ranks of the Rhode Island Militia and included the Newport Artillery, active since 1741, and the First Light Infantry, which had stormed Acote's Hill during the Dorr Rebellion:

- Company A: Providence "National Cadets"
- Company B: Providence "Providence Artillery"
- Company C: Providence "First Light Infantry"
- Company D: Providence "First Light Infantry"
- Company E: Pawtucket "Pawtucket Light Guard"
- Company F: Newport "Newport Artillery"
- Company G: Providence "Mechanics Rifles"

- Company H: Providence "Mechanics Rifles"
- Company I: Westerly "Westerly Rifles"
- Company K: Woonsocket "Woonsocket Light Guard"

The Rhode Islanders appeared in "business-like attire," a uniform designed by Burnside consisting of a baggy pull-over shirt, gray trousers and a red blanket that doubled as a poncho. The red blankets, supplied by the Sprague Mills in Cranston, were issued to many Rhode Islanders. On the way south, the regiment had to go by water to Washington, as the Baltimore Depot had been closed since the riots of April 19. Traveling to Annapolis, the regiment became the subject of a popular early war song, "Nine Miles to the Junction."

The regiment arrived in Washington and, without quarters, was housed in the Patent Office before the men built Camp Sprague, eventually becoming the rendezvous point for Rhode Island units on their way to the seat of war. Many of the soldiers in the regiment were the sons of the elite and wealthy of Rhode Island and believed that this was their one chance to gain military glory to further their careers later in life. As such, cargoes of ice and fresh provisions were shipped south to the camp, and President Lincoln was a frequent visitor at Camp Sprague. Despite the elite status of the regiment, it did not prevent Private Henry C. Davis, a seventeen-year-old from Woonsocket, from becoming the first Rhode Islander to die in the Civil War, perishing from disease on June 16, 1861.

Chaplain Augustus Woodbury remembered the regiment's first march to Harpers Ferry:

> On the 10th of June, the regiment marched on an expedition towards Harper's Ferry, preceded the day before by the Battery attached to it, to join other forces under General Patterson, for the purpose of dislodging the rebels under General Joseph E. Johnston, then holding that place. The expedition was accompanied to Greencastle by Ex-Governor Dyer, of Providence, who rendered timely and efficient service. The Regiment was here joined by Governor Sprague, accompanied by his Aide-de-Camp, Colonel John A. Gardner. It advanced to Williamsport, in the State of Maryland, but the evacuation of Harper's Ferry by General Johnston rendered the further prosecution of the campaign unnecessary, and in obedience to orders received from Washington, the Regiment returned to that city, and on the 20th of June was established once more at Camp Sprague. The excessive heat and clouds of dust rendered the marching on

William Rathbun of East Greenwich (right) lost his leg trying to help his wounded friend Oliver Dowd off the battlefield at Fredericksburg.

*this expedition exceedingly fatiguing, but the discomforts were borne with cheerfulness. It was on this occasion that the Regiment made a march of thirty-three miles in a single day, and "in half an hour from the time the head of the column arrived at the encampment, every straggler had found his proper place in his company bivouac.*

After the advance into the Shenandoah Valley, the regiment returned to Camp Sprague, where the men welcomed their brothers from the Second Rhode Island Volunteers.

Together with the Second Rhode Island Battery, the Second New Hampshire and Seventy-first New York, they composed Burnside's Brigade. On June 16, 1861, the Rhode Islanders led the advance to Bull Run. For many it was the time of their lives, leisurely walking through the Virginia countryside, unaware of what awaited them on the morning of July 21 at Matthew's Hill, near Manassas, Virginia. The regiment was held in reserve as Burnside deployed the Second Rhode Island. Forty-five minutes later, the First Rhode Island finally went in, changing front under fire as it deployed to the support of the Second, creating a long line of 1,500 Rhode Islanders. Enemy fire began to hit the regiment, but the men held on. Among those hit was Theodore Wheaton King of Newport, the son of a wealthy doctor. Captured by the enemy, he died in captivity; in his memory, his parents erected a large monument to him in Island Cemetery. With another brigade on the field and the Rhode Islanders out of ammunition, they were pulled off the line but quickly joined in the panicked retreat back to Washington. Instead of retreating, Dr. James Harris, the assistant surgeon, stayed with his patients, allowing himself to be captured instead of abandoning them. Nearly thirty men were captured in the retreat, while several died in prison at Richmond.

A week after Bull Run, the First returned to Rhode Island. Although it only served for three months, the regiment had a well-earned reputation for its quick response in April 1861, and 60 percent of the men reenlisted, serving as officers in all of Rhode Island's other regiments. In 1862, Chaplain Augustus Woodbury published *A Narrative of the Campaign of the First Rhode Island in the Spring and Summer of 1861*. The first published regimental history, it set the standard by which hundreds have been written over the last century and a half.

*Battle Honors: Bull Run.*

# SECOND RHODE ISLAND VOLUNTEERS

In his postwar history on combat losses in the Civil War, Lieutenant Colonel William F. Fox correctly called the Second Rhode Island Volunteers "Rhode Island's Fighting Regiment." Few other regiments could claim that they had fought from Bull Run to Appomattox. Among the men of this regiment was a young soldier who rose from private to colonel and became the voice of the common soldier of the North via Ken Burns's *The Civil War*: Elisha Hunt Rhodes. The companies of the Second were recruited from the following Rhode Island communities in May 1861:

- Company A: Warwick
- Company B: Cranston, Foster and Scituate
- Company C: Providence
- Company D: Providence
- Company E: South Kingstown

- Company F: Pawtucket
- Company G: Bristol
- Company H: East Greenwich
- Company I: Glocester and Smithfield
- Company K: Newport

The original colonel of the Second was John Stanton Slocum. He had distinguished himself during the Mexican-American War, earning a brevet at Chapultepec. He was originally the major of the First Rhode Island but was transferred to the Second when it was created. Slocum's lieutenant colonel was Frank Wheaton, a veteran of five years' service on the frontier with the First Cavalry. Hastily formed, the Second left for the front in June 1861, bound for Camp Sprague.

The Second Rhode Island followed the Union forces to Bull Run in July 1861. Colonel Slocum asked Burnside to assign his regiment to the front, which he did. To a fellow officer he quipped, "Today victory and a star, or a soldier's grave." It was the men of Company E, soldiers from South Kingstown, who first made contact with Confederate forces at Matthew's Hill, firing the first infantry shots of the battle. Slocum ordered up the rest of his regiment. An eyewitness recalled the opening fight:

> *They come from the shots, the factories, the farms, the schools, scattered all over our little State, but they are of sturdy New England ancestry. These are the men, this is the leader* [Slocum], *who so promptly formed in line and faced the enemy upon the crest of the hill beyond the ford, and opened the sanguinary engagement of Manassas Plain! This is the regiment, this is the colonel, who stood a full half hour,* alone *against Georgia, Alabama, and South Carolina, till ammunition and physical strength were exhausted, yet stubbornly refusing to yield to the ever-increasing foe the crest so gallantly won!*

As Colonel Slocum mounted a fence, he turned to his men and shouted, "Now show them what Rhode Island can do!" Seconds later, he was struck in the head and died two days later. The brave colonel's remains were recovered in March and interred in Swan Point Cemetery. In 1886, the Rhode Island Grand Army of the Republic erected a large monument over his burial site. At the same time Slocum fell, Major Sullivan Ballou, famous for the last letter he may or may not have written, was mortally wounded as well. His body was later dug up by men from Georgia, beheaded and burned as an

First Sergeant James C. Nichols, Company B, Second Rhode Island, from Scituate, served and was killed at Chancellorsville.

act of revenge against the destruction rendered by the Second Rhode Island on the Eighth Georgia. One Georgian brought his skull back to Savannah to use as a punchbowl; all that was ever found of Major Ballou was his shirt and some charred bones.

With the help of the First Rhode Island, the Second finally cleared Matthew's Hill but retreated when it ran out of ammunition and was being pursued by the Rebels. In its first fight, the Second lost thirty-two men killed, fifty-six wounded and thirty captured. Lieutenant Colonel Wheaton became the colonel, with officers below him moving up as well.

Returning to Washington, the Second spent the winter of 1861–62 at Camp Brightwood, constructing Fort Slocum north of the city. Assigned to what eventually became the Sixth Corps, the Second went to the Peninsula in the spring of 1862. Arriving on the Peninsula, the soldiers had an interesting experience on picket duty, seeing Georgians with equipment looted from the Rhode Island dead at Bull Run. The regiment was largely held in reserve on the Peninsula, only seeing major combat during a reconnaissance in force at Seven Pines. The Second was again held in reserve at Antietam and Fredericksburg. In December, Colonel Wheaton was promoted to brigadier general.

# The Infantry

Under the command of Horatio Rogers, the Second fought at Chancellorsville in May 1863. The regiment advanced from Fredericksburg in good order but ran against a brigade of Alabamians at Salem's Church. Caught in a murderous crossfire, soldiers fell by the score. First Sergeant James Nichols of Scituate was killed instantly by a shot to the head; after the war, the veterans of the town dedicated the Grand Army of the Republic Hall to his memory. Colonel Rogers recalled, as the Confederates hid behind a fence, "Our boys lay as flat to mother earth as they could get." The Rebels tried to outflank the regiment, but Rogers sent three companies into the woods to refuse the regiment's left flank. Rogers then saw that the Twenty-sixth New Jersey was in trouble, and as he later remembered, "Never was a man more glad to see another than was that New Jersey colonel to see the Rhode Island one." The Second held on until some Vermonters came up to lend support as well. Although heavily bloodied at Salem's Church, the Sixth Corps pulled back the next day to Banks' Ford and retreated.

After Chancellorsville, the Second made an epic march to Gettysburg but only came under stray artillery fire, losing one man killed and another five wounded. Although not as heavily engaged in this battle as others, the veterans returned to the field after the war, erecting a monument near Little Round Top to mark their location. Going into camp at Brandy Station that winter, Colonel Rogers resigned and returned home to become attorney general. The Second Rhode Island moved forward with the Army of the Potomac in the spring of 1864. At the Wilderness, Spotsylvania and Cold Harbor, the Second was heavily engaged, losing half of its strength in the thickets and woodlots south of the Rapidan River. Private Charles Nichols of Hopkinton wrote about his experience in the Wilderness:

> *The fourth time they charge up, they came in solid column on, on they came with form and steady step, our musketry sweeping their ranks to be instantly filled presenting a solid front. As they neared us and were within 10 rods some of the Regiments gave way, but the 2nd RI stood firm, although heavily pressed. Just at this time in my immediate front and in advance of the rest was a large and portly man. I sighted him and fired. As I took my gun from my shoulder, he threw both hands across his stomach and rolled up like a fry cake. I at once turned partly round to load as quickly as possible, and when a ball passed through my left shoulder and threw me to the ground and when I arose, another struck me in the back, about an inch from the lower part of the spine. This took me down again. When I was*

Elisha Hunt Rhodes of the Second Rhode Island retold his story of the Civil War through a popular journal aired as part of Ken Burns's *The Civil War*.

*seized by Lewis and carried me to the rear, some 4 or 5 rods. Libby and Andersonville Prisons were staring me in the face, such was the feelings of horror came over me.*

Reported as killed to his family, Nichols was sent home to Hope Valley to recover and became a successful businessman after the war, helping to write a history of his regiment.

On the morning of June 11, as the regiment was in line of battle at Cold Harbor, those few survivors who had made it through their three-year enlistment were mustered out and sent home. Captain Elisha Hunt Rhodes, who rose from private, was placed in command of a consolidated battalion of three companies. In the fall of 1864, Governor Smith, not wanting the regiment to be combined with the Seventh Rhode Island, authorized the recruiting of five new companies to bring the regiment back up to strength.

A severely understrength Second Rhode Island arrived at Petersburg in June 1864 but, two weeks later, joined the Sixth Corps at Fort Stevens and then pursued the Confederates into the Shenandoah Valley, fighting at Opequon in mid-September. Assigned to garrison Winchester, the unit missed the fighting at Fisher's Hill and Cedar Creek. The Second returned to the Petersburg siege lines in January 1865, as the new recruits prepared for the spring campaign. On the morning of April 2, 1865, with Lieutenant Colonel Rhodes in the lead, the Second left the entrenchments and charged into Petersburg. The two color-bearers, Sergeant William J. Babcock and Corporal Thomas Parker, earned two of the nine Medals of Honor awarded to Rhode Islanders that day.

Four days later, the Second was heavily engaged in the rear-guard action at Sailor's Creek. Captain Charles Gleason of Coventry became the last Rhode Island officer to lose his life in combat. Three days later, the Second Rhode Island, the men who had fired the opening shots of the Battle of Bull Run, were there as well for the last, at Appomattox Court House. The regiment returned to Rhode Island in July and was mustered out.

*Battle Honors: Bull Run, Williamsburg, Malvern Hill, Antietam, Fredericksburg, Marye's Heights, Salem's Heights, Gettysburg, Rappahannock Station, Wilderness, Spotsylvania, Cold Harbor, Petersburg, Fort Stevens, Opequon, Storming of Petersburg, Sailor's Creek and Appomattox.*

# FOURTH RHODE ISLAND VOLUNTEERS

The Fourth Rhode Island was the last full infantry unit raised in Rhode Island in 1861. After Union setbacks at Bull Run, the regiment had no trouble recruiting ten companies from every corner of Rhode Island in September. The companies were recruited as follows:

- Company A: Providence
- Company B: Providence
- Company C: Providence
- Company D: Burrillville, Glocester and Hopkinton
- Company E: Woonsocket
- Company F: Providence
- Company G: Middletown and Newport
- Company H: North Kingstown
- Company I: Pawtucket
- Company K: Warwick

Only seventeen years old, Private Charles Baker of Wickford, a member of Company H, Fourth Rhode Island, died in the Fourth's charge at New Berne.

General Isaac Peace Rodman
of South Kingstown was the
highest-ranking Rhode Islander
to die in the Civil War.

The regiment was originally commanded by Isaac Peace Rodman of South Kingstown. Although often written, Rodman was not a Quaker but rather a devout Baptist whose family mills in Peace Dale were beginning to suffer from the lack of raw materials from the South. Raising a company of fellow South Kingstown men for the Second Rhode Island, Rodman distinguished himself at Bull Run and was promoted from captain to colonel of the new regiment.

Originally sent to Washington, the Fourth soon joined Ambrose Burnside at Annapolis as part of his "Coast Division," which later formed the nucleus of the Ninth Corps. Sailing to the coast of North Carolina, the Fourth participated in the Battle of Roanoke Island that February. On March 14, 1862, as Union forces approached the city of New Berne, the division came under heavy enemy fire. Colonel Rodman saw a gap in the Confederate line and ordered a bayonet charge. Rodman's men surged forward, capturing several pieces of artillery and the guidon of Latham's Battery and routing the Confederate troops. In his after-action report, Burnside credited the Fourth as being the reason the Union troops won the battle; Burnside earned a second star, while Rodman became a brigadier general. Following New Berne, the Fourth participated in the Siege of Fort Macon.

In late August, the Fourth moved north to Newport News, Virginia. Here Governor William Sprague appointed Lieutenant Colonel W.H.P.

Steere of the Second Rhode Island to the vacant colonelcy of the regiment, sidestepping Lieutenant Colonel William Tew of the Fourth. When the news reached the regiment, two-thirds of the officers resigned on the spot, while the new colonel was physically assaulted by his men as they mutinied, failing to respond to his commands. An angry Governor Sprague personally went to Newport News to settle the situation, commissioning new officers and placing Captain Joseph B. Curtis as second in command. With the new officers, the regiment slowly marched north into Maryland in pursuit of Lee's army.

On September 17, 1862, at Antietam, the Fourth fought a terrible engagement in Otto's Cornfield, a forty-acre entanglement on the southern edge of the battlefield. The regiment formed the extreme left flank of the Army of the Potomac. Unable to locate the enemy in the dense corn, a picket soon made contact, and the color-bearer was killed. The Fourth Rhode Island quickly engaged the foe, but the enemy soon gained the exposed left flank. Corporal George Allen recalled, "Our men fell like sheep at the slaughter." Josiah and Jeremiah Moon were twin brothers from Coventry who marched side by side that day; Josiah was killed by the side of his twin. Colonel Steere fell early in the fight as scores of his men were shot down.

Corporal Benjamin F. Burdick of Hopkinton died trying to save his boyhood friend Isaac Freeman Saunders. The Sixteenth Connecticut, a newly organized unit whose men had not even had time to learn how to load their muskets, broke and retreated, leaving the Fourth to face an entire Confederate brigade by itself. General Rodman tried to rally the line but was shot in the chest and died two weeks later, becoming the highest-ranking Rhode Island officer to die in the Civil War. Finally, the Fourth had no choice but to retreat, leaving nearly thirty dead and seventy wounded in the cornfield.

Three months later, at Fredericksburg, the Fourth was again under fire, where Lieutenant Colonel Curtis became the only fatality. As the regiment formed up to attack Marye's Heights, a lieutenant in Battery D reminded the men, "Boys, Remember that old Rhode Island is looking at you to-day." A witty private in the ranks, watching the battle unfold to the front, replied, "By jabbers we'd rather be looking at Rhode Island about these times."

The regiment spent most of 1863 and 1864 garrisoning a line of fortifications near Suffolk, Virginia, occasionally coming under fire. In the winter of 1864, the unit guarded Confederate prisoners at Point Lookout, Maryland. Returned to the Ninth Corps in July 1864, the Fourth began losing men immediately in the trenches before Petersburg. Three Myrick brothers from Coventry had volunteered in the fall of 1861. Private Samuel

Myrick was killed at New Berne, while his older brother, Sergeant Cromwell P. Myrick, died at Petersburg, leaving Solomon Myrick alone to return home and mourn the loss of not only his comrades but his brothers as well.

On July 30, 1864, the Fourth advanced on the city during the fiasco that was known as the Battle of the Crater. Pinned down in "the horrid pit," half the regiment became casualties, with many choosing capture instead of risking their lives in running away. When the United States flag went down, Private James Welsh of Smithfield grasped the colors and ran back toward the Union line, earning the Medal of Honor. The Crater was the last major engagement for the Fourth, now reduced to barely one hundred men; the regiment was largely held in reserve the rest of the summer.

On the morning of September 30, 1864, as the Fourth was in the process of mustering out, the regiment volunteered to go into combat one last time. Advancing toward Poplar Spring Church, a shell exploded in the midst of the color guard, killing 3 members on the eve of their departure from the front. The following day, the regiment returned to Rhode Island. Nearly 150 officers and the men who had reenlisted remained in the field and were consolidated with the Seventh Rhode Island, helping to bolster the low strength of that regiment. The new title did not sit too well with the veterans, who nearly mutinied again. Corporal Allen recalled in later years, "We were *once* and *always*, the Fourth Rhode Island Regiment."

*Battle Honors: Roanoke Island, New Berne, Fort Macon, South Mountain, Antietam, Fredericksburg, Suffolk, Petersburg, Weldon Railroad, Hatcher's Run and Poplar Spring Church.*

# SEVENTH RHODE ISLAND VOLUNTEERS

Of the eight infantry regiments that Rhode Island fielded during the Civil War, the Seventh Rhode Island traveled farther and lost more men than any other unit. Orders to raise the regiment were issued in May 1862, but it was not until July that a serious recruitment effort got underway. Some towns such as Scituate and Hopkinton offered bounties of $400 for men to enlist, while South Kingstown offered $500. The funds, combined with a serious call from President Lincoln for 300,000 volunteers in July 1862, led men to the cause. The ten companies of the Seventh came from the following communities:

- Company A: Charlestown, Hopkinton and Richmond
- Company B: Providence
- Company C: Glocester
- Company D: Burrillville and West Greenwich
- Company E: Cumberland, Smithfield and Woonsocket
- Company F: Exeter and North Kingstown
- Company G: South Kingstown
- Company H: East Greenwich and Warwick
- Company I: Newport and Bristol
- Company K: Coventry, Foster and Scituate

The soldiers who served in the Seventh could not have had a better officer to lead them. Colonel Zenas R. Bliss was a West Pointer from the class of 1854, had served six years on the plains and had recently returned from a stint leading the Tenth Rhode Island. Drawing largely from the western and southern parts of Rhode Island, the Seventh left the state in September 1862 and spent several weeks in the defenses of Washington before permanent assignment to the Ninth Corps.

The Seventh was baptized at Fredericksburg on December 13, 1862. Shortly before the battle, Major Jacob Babbitt, a fifty-three-year-old banker from Bristol, wrote a touching letter to his wife: "Should it be my lot to fall, know that it was in defense of my beloved Constitution." The regiment rushed headlong toward an entrenched Confederate foe on Marye's Heights, losing men for every bit of ground gained, including Major Babbitt, who was shot in the chest and died a week later. Every member of the regimental staff was killed or wounded, while Colonel Bliss earned the Medal of Honor for his leadership by picking up the musket from a fallen soldier and joining his men on the firing line. Private Abel B. Kenyon, a millworker from Hopkinton who had joined up with his two brothers-in-law, Isaac N. Saunders and J. Weeden Burdick, wrote:

*Camp near Frederick Burg, Va. Dec 26. 1862*
*Brother Benjamin,*

*I received your letter last night and was glad to hear from you though you did not say in particular whether you were all sick or well. I take it that you are all well at least I hope so we boys are all well as usuall and I feel verry thankful for it you spoke of the 7 Reg being in the Battle I think it*

First Sergeant Charles H. Kellen was a young teacher from Providence when he joined Company F, Seventh Rhode Island, in the summer of 1862. He was mortally wounded at Fredericksburg.

*was and in a warm one we marched over the river sixth day morning and lay around in the streat that day and night & seaventh day morning the shells bursted closte to us one bursted within 12 feet of me & killed one man & wounded another you had better believe that the boys began to look around themselves we stood that until about noon then we started for the field there was nothing said but a good deal of thinking if rest was like me I can tell you that the canon balls and rifle ballls come thick and fast when we was going on to the field but we went up in good line though we had to walk over many dead and wounded men we loded our pieces on our knees and lying down I rose and fired and layed down again we was in line on the field about five hours until after dark the rifle balls sounded just like a swarm of bees huming around the hive we marched off the field back to the citty about ½ mile into the old building any where we could for the night our Col. Bliss said to us he did not feel like making a speech but he would say to us we had the honor of doing the best of any Regiment on the field it was a sad time any way we can fix it such a time I never want to see again but verry likely we shall see more fighting if we do I hope the Lord will be with us and carry us safe through & be permitted to return home once more and see you all again I dont want you to send them boots until we send for them tell Julia I want a vest made something cheap that will be warm I have not time nor paper to rite more so I will close by sending my respecks to you all write soon.*

*Abel B. Kenyon*

*I would like to have a little money they have not paid us off yet and dont know as they ever will I want Government money if you have any let Julia see this and the old folks I havent got any paper to write her as soon as I can get some I will write. Yours ever A.B.K.*

Private Alfred Sheldon Knight of Scituate recalled, "The balls and shells fell like hail around us." With fences blocking their way, the regiment clambered to within seventy-five yards of the Confederate line before the men fell back, with a New York regiment cheering them on. The regiment lost 47 dead and more than 150 wounded—the most men ever lost by a Rhode Island unit in any battle of any war. Captain Lewis Leavens of Hopkinton recalled, "Scarce but a man lost a friend or relative." When the list of casualties in South Kingstown was reported, the local paper could barely keep up with the bad news.

Following Fredericksburg, the shattered regiment spent a miserable, disease-filled winter at Falmouth, Virginia, losing heavily to typhoid, dysentery and pneumonia; among the dead was Private Alfred S. Knight, who died of pneumonia on January 31, 1863. In March, the regiment was transferred with the Ninth Corps to Newport News and then in April to Kentucky. From here, it was sent in June to reinforce Union forces at Vicksburg. Engaged in a rear-guard action at Jackson, Mississippi, the Seventh lost more than fifty men to disease contracted in Mississippi. Among them was J. Weeden Burdick, one of the most popular men in Company A, who died of a mysterious illness, called "Yazoo Fever," that plagued many of the men. Sergeant Winfield S. Chappell of South Kingstown wrote:

*The Mississippi Campaign was one of hardship and suffering. The heat was awful and the water at best was no better. We left many of our Company in Miss., poor boys. They have gone and I trust they are in a happier world. That we were sorrowful at there loss wil not in no means begin with our feelings. It was hard for us, very hard indeed, and thousands of times have I thought of them and mourned their loss. Oh, think only a*

# The Infantry

*little more than a year ago they left their homes full of life and hope with the expectation of returning. Their hopes are blasted and their bodies now rest in Southern soil.*

After returning to Kentucky in late August with only one hundred men able to bear arms, the regiment spent the winter on picket duty, recovering from the tortuous ordeal.

Returning to Virginia in the spring of 1864, after spending a winter of picket duty fighting guerrillas in Kentucky, the Seventh was in reserve at the Wilderness, but from May 12 onward it was constantly engaged under fire during the Overland Campaign. On May 12, 1864, in a driving rainstorm at Spotsylvania Court House, the regiment helped to save the faltering Union line. It was a hard day for the small mill community of Rockville in Hopkinton, as Privates Isaac Saunders and Benjamin Sisson were killed; today they are buried side by side at Fredericksburg National Cemetery. Meanwhile, Abel Kenyon was shot in the hand while loading his rifle. The only one of his brothers-in-law to survive the war, he returned to his wife, Julia, the sister of Weeden Burdick, and lived a long life. The Seventh remained under fire for a week at Spotsylvania.

On May 18, the regiment again charged the Confederate line; one shell killed or injured 6 men from Warwick. A terse struggle in command left the regiment under the leadership of twenty-one-year-old Lieutenant Colonel Percy Daniels, an immature, reckless leader, instead of in the hands of a more senior officer. Daniels had obtained the position through political patronage. Fighting again at the North Anna River in late May, the Seventh advanced to Cold Harbor on June 3. With only 150 men in line, they charged a heavily entrenched Confederate force near a swamp at Bethesda Church; more than one-third of the men fell in the desperate assault. Corporal Nathan B. Lewis of Exeter took 14 men into action with Company F, and only half came back. Arriving at Petersburg in mid-June, there were fewer than 80 men in line, while Company H literally had 1 man left. Pulled off the line as combat troops, the regiment served as engineers, helping to strengthen the Union line by constructing fortifications. The unit further distinguished itself at the Battle of the Crater, forming a strong skirmish line to support the Union retreat.

In September, the Seventh again fought at Poplar Spring Church, holding the Rebels in check until the Union line could regroup. The regiment then moved to Fort Sedgwick, ably named by Seventh soldiers "Fort Hell" for its proximity to the Confederate line; the pickets were so close that they could talk to one another in normal tones of voice. The men literally lived underground in soggy, mud-filled holes called "bombproofs." The Seventh's last battle was during the Storming of Petersburg on April 2, 1865. Bringing ammunition to the troops on the front line, the Seventh again proved itself under fire, losing several officers and men. On June 9, 1865, the Seventh Rhode Island Volunteers was mustered out of service and returned to Rhode Island after marching thousands of miles and fighting battles in three states.

After the war, the soldiers of the Seventh carried on the comradeship they enjoyed in the army by forming one of Rhode Island's first veterans organizations, writing a regimental history and dedicating a regimental monument at Vicksburg in 1908. The last survivor of the regiment, Private Elisha Watson of Coventry, died in 1939.

*Battle Honors: Fredericksburg, Vicksburg, Jackson, Spotsylvania, North Anna, Cold Harbor, Petersburg, Weldon Railroad, Hatcher's Run and Poplar Spring Church.*

# NINTH RHODE ISLAND VOLUNTEERS

The Ninth and Tenth Rhode Island Volunteers were three-month regiments raised in May 1862 to serve in the defenses of Washington at a time when it was feared that Stonewall Jackson's Confederates, operating in the Shenandoah Valley, would break through the Union defenses and attack Washington. Hastily raised from militia companies from throughout Rhode Island, the Ninth was unique because it contained eleven companies rather than the standard ten. The unit was recruited as follows:

- Company A: Pawtucket "Pawtucket Light Guard"
- Company B: Westerly "Westerly Rifles"
- Company C: Warwick "Natick National Guard"
- Company D: Pawtucket "Pawtucket National Guard"
- Company E: Pawtucket "Pawtucket National Guard"
- Company F: Smithfield "Lonsdale National Guard"
- Company G: Woonsocket "Woonsocket Light Guard"
- Company H: Pawtucket "Slater Drill Corps"
- Company I: Warren

- Company K: Providence
- Company L: Newport

Because the regiment only served for three months, and then only in the defenses of Washington on picket and fatigue duty, it did not leave behind a remarkable record, other than the fact that it was recruited and on its way to the front within forty hours of receiving the call. Commanding the regiment was John T. Pitman, a veteran of the Dorr Rebellion and the First Rhode Island, who brought his son to war with him.

The Ninth Rhode Island spent its entire term of service in garrison at Washington, allowing many to pass a hot but interesting summer away from home. Sergeant Henry Richardson of Company H spent much of his free time wandering around the Capitol and the Smithsonian. During the brief service, three men died of disease. The Ninth Rhode Island returned home in late August 1862. Although not engaged in battle, the soldiers of the Ninth eagerly answered the call and were ready to go to the front, but they waited for orders that never came.

*Battle Honors: None.*

# Tenth Rhode Island Volunteers

Much like the Ninth Rhode Island, the Tenth was a three-month unit quickly raised in May 1862. The entire regiment was recruited from the various wards of Providence. The Tenth was commanded by Zenas Randall Bliss of Johnston, who had just returned home after a year in a Confederate prison. Bliss rebuffed the offer at first, wanting to return to his Regular Army regiment, but when told that he could have command of the Seventh Regiment once it was full, Bliss relented. He led his men to Washington, where like the Ninth they garrisoned the forts around the city. Company B of the Tenth was composed largely of students from Brown University, commanded by Elisha Dyer, a former Rhode Island governor. On the night of June 16, Dyer and his men captured a small Confederate cannon that is still in the possession of the Rhode Island National Guard.

Throughout the rest of the summer, the troops labored to build an extensive series of fortifications north of the city, often in one-hundred-degree heat. Colonel Bliss left the regiment in August to return home to command the Seventh and was replaced by James Shaw. On the eve of Second Bull Run, as the Confederates were only miles from the city, Shaw and his men left to return to Rhode Island, much to the disgust of the War Department, which asked them to stay a week longer to protect the capital. Rather, the colonel and his men believed that they had done their duty and that the newly arriving troops could handle the situation. Like the Ninth, three men died of disease. On September 1, 1862, the Tenth was mustered out the service. Surprisingly, many of the Brown students from Company B put their studies on hold and returned to the army in other Rhode Island units.

*Battle Honors: None.*

# ELEVENTH RHODE ISLAND VOLUNTEERS

By August 1862, the Union war effort had stalled, with forces in the East and West at a standstill. President Lincoln believed that if 300,000 fresh troops were thrown into the field immediately, the rebellion might be over by Christmas. As such, he called for that number of men to serve for nine months. In Rhode Island, two regiments, the Eleventh and Twelfth Rhode Island Volunteers, were called for. The Eleventh was raised in the communities listed here:

- Company A: Providence
- Company B: Pawtucket
- Company C: Providence
- Company D: Providence
- Company E: Providence
- Company F: Pawtucket
- Company G: Providence
- Company H: Providence
- Company I: Providence
- Company K: Providence

Two companies of the regiment were raised by the YMCA in Providence, while Company K was composed largely of the students of high school

Munro Gladding, a quartermaster in the Fifth Rhode Island, died of disease in North Carolina.

teacher Captain Charles Mowry. Soldiers who had enlisted for three years and received $100 in bounty money became severely upset when their comrades at home earned nearly $250 for nine months' service. The regiment first marched in the funeral of General Rodman, who died at Antietam, before leaving the state in early October for Washington.

The Eleventh was originally commanded by Colonel Edwin Metcalf, who left a month later to command the Third Rhode Island; he was replaced by Horatio Rogers, who left as well to command the Second Rhode Island. Finally, George Church, the hated lieutenant colonel of the Seventh Rhode Island, was promoted in February 1863. Originally assigned to guard a convalescent camp around Washington, the men were eager for action. Private Ansel Nichols of Pawtucket passed his time writing letters to the *Pawtucket Gazette* about his wartime experiences. Much of the time was spent in camp on picket duty, trying to cope with a tough Virginia winter. The mother of Private Joseph Padelford nagged him to write more letters home, but to this the young soldier replied, "You complain about my not writing oftener. If I was to write one every day there would be but one a month or one to every seven I write answered. I have sent home three and have not heard from either of them. In my last I sent a cheque for Sixty Dollars on the state Commissioner I don't know whether you have received it or not."

Finally, in mid-April 1863, the Eleventh got its chance to go to the front. After much pleading by Colonel Church, the Eleventh was sent to Suffolk, Virginia, where it joined the Fourth Rhode Island. For the next two months, the regiment trudged between Suffolk, Norfolk and Yorktown, constantly expecting an engagement that never came. In its one skirmish, one private was slightly wounded, while nine men died of disease. Finally, on July 6, 1863, the Eleventh returned to Providence and was mustered out.

*Battle Honors: Suffolk.*

# TWELFTH RHODE ISLAND VOLUNTEERS

The Twelfth Rhode Island was recruited at the same time as the Eleventh Rhode Island to serve for nine months. Unlike the Eleventh, the Twelfth joined the Army of the Potomac and met with disastrous results. The unit was recruited from the following communities:

- Company A: recruited at large
- Company B: Cranston
- Company C: Johnston and Providence
- Company D: New Shoreham and Newport
- Company E: Barrington, Bristol and Warren
- Company F: Cumberland
- Company G: Coventry and Tiverton
- Company H: North Providence
- Company I: Warwick
- Company K: Burrillville

Company D included the only organized contingent of men to serve from Block Island; of the sixteen soldiers who joined, six died in the army. From the beginning, the Twelfth was a poorly organized and poorly equipped regiment. The colonel was George H. Browne of Chepachet. Browne had no formal military training. He was, however, the Democratic congressman from Rhode Island's Second District. By appointing him to command, Sprague would guarantee that a Republican could capture the seat that fall. In addition to Browne's failings, only three of the commissioned officers had ever seen active duty, while the regiment was armed with outdated smoothbore muskets. These factors all led to a series of breakdowns that eventually handicapped the command.

Even before leaving Rhode Island, the troops protested in Providence that they were not paid the proper bounty, resulting in a militia company threatening to open fire if the men did not return to camp. Colonel Browne finally got his men aboard a train that proceeded to place the regiment on guard duty at Fairfax Seminary, Virginia, where they picketed until late November. Later that month, the Rhode Islanders were called to join the First Brigade, Second Division, Ninth Corps, encamped before Fredericksburg. Private Frank J. Wilder of Scituate wrote of the march and subsequent battle:

*Tuesday Dec. 23rd 1862*
*Camp before Fredericksburg.*

*Frend Asa.*

*I have been thinking of writing to you for some time but have had so much to do that I could not find time. We have been out on Brigade review to day and have just got back and eat our dinner of bean soup and hard bread a tip top dish you better believe. We had a pretty hard march from Fairfax Seminary to Fredericksburg about 120 miles by the way we came and when we had got here they shoved us right into battle and thinned us out considerable we lost 25 men killed and wounded in our company Wm Harris got wounded pretty bad but Wm Hopkins came out safe and so did I with the exception of a bruise on my shoulder they give us enough of it there and I guess there are not many here that want to get into the same place again. We have pretty good times n camp generally there is something going on all the time which makes a fellow feel contended with his lot. I expect we shall go into winter quarters before long if we dont get into another battle. We are in camp right along side the 7th Regt and I believe we are brigaded with them. We have been out on picket in front of the rebel lines and since we have been here and we could see plenty of them. I expect you are having some pretty cold weather there now we dont have such cold weather down here. There is not much news to write about out here and I guess I will close*

*give my respcts to all the boys and tell them to write to me write soon and*
*give me all the news from*

*your friend*
*Frank J. Wilder*

Assigned to storm Marye's Heights alongside the Seventh Rhode Island, it was baptism by fire for both regiments. The Seventh, under a veteran commander, pressed forward toward the hill, losing heavily, while the Twelfth floundered. Major Cyrus Dyer, Browne's only other field officer, was wounded early in the fight as part of the regiment became bogged down in a railroad cut. The right wing tried to press on, but a deadly crossfire hit the regiment. First by squads and then companies, finally the entire Twelfth Rhode Island ran away from the scene of action, the men throwing away their equipment as they ran back to the city. Twenty men died and more than eighty were wounded in the disastrous engagement. After the war, the veterans of the Twelfth were successful in promoting themselves as brave defenders of the Republic, covering up what had actually happened. Many Rhode Island soldiers from the time were disgusted by what the regiment did, sending home reports in many letters after Fredericksburg.

Following Fredericksburg, the Twelfth joined the Seventh at the Falmouth encampment, losing severely to disease; among the dead was Private Wilder. Their respite came in March, when the two regiments and the Ninth Corps were transferred to Newport News, receiving much-needed supplies. The bad reputation of the Twelfth continued here as well, with the regiment engaging in a violent fight with the Forty-eighth Pennsylvania.

In April, the Twelfth was transferred to Kentucky, where it earned the colorful title of the "Trotting Twelfth," for the five hundred miles the men marched around the state in a short period of time. When the Seventh Rhode Island went to Vicksburg in June 1863, the Twelfth remained in Kentucky, performing guard duty and occasionally engaging Confederate cavalry. The reputation of the regiment continued as the men constantly drank the Kentucky bourbon, and one man was murdered by a local. Finally, in July 1863, after remaining on duty for several weeks during John Morgan's Ohio Raid, the regiment returned to Rhode Island for muster out.

Private Albert Perry of Richmond, who served in the Seventh Rhode Island, wrote, "Never let them bring that shame upon ther flag and upon the state that the 12th Rhode Island did. Altho they are at home now and we are glad for them and we can tell them one thing that is they are not thought of much of in our Brigade they was tip top blowers but darn poor feighters."

*Battle Honors: Fredericksburg.*


# Hospital Guards


Perhaps the most interesting Rhode Island unit to never see combat was the Rhode Island Hospital Guards. While most Civil War recruits had to pass a strict (for the time) medical examination, the Hospital Guards looked for men who could not serve in the field. The company, eventually numbering nearly one hundred men, was stationed at Lovell General Hospital in Portsmouth, Grove. Here the unit acted as a military police force, guarding the camp, preventing desertion and escorting men back to their units. While never under fire, the men were constantly on guard duty, even in the winter, as they struggled to cope with the harsh elements of their New England home.

*Battle Honors: None.*

# Chapter 3

# The Cavalry

## FIRST RHODE ISLAND CAVALRY

The origins of the First Rhode Island Cavalry are as interesting as the history of the regiment itself. In the fall of 1861, the New England states had yet to raise any cavalry regiments. Governor Sprague had the idea to form a "New England Cavalry Regiment" composed of two companies from each of the six New England states. The governors of Massachusetts, Vermont, Maine, New Hampshire and Connecticut were enthusiastic about the plan as well, hoping that a mounted regiment would spurn enlistments. The cavalry plan was so successful that each state but Rhode Island and New Hampshire raised a full regiment. Rhode Island raised eight companies, recruited at large from all corners of the state, while four companies from New Hampshire joined to create the First New England Cavalry. The War Department did not support the regional recruitment plan. As such, in 1862 the regiment became the First Rhode Island, much to the disgust of the New Hampshiremen. In 1863, the surviving New Hampshire troopers returned to the Granite State to form to the nucleus of the First New Hampshire Cavalry.

Going into camp at Pawtucket, the men were armed with Burnside carbines and rode Morgan horses from Vermont. They left Rhode Island in January 1862 and were quickly ordered into the Shenandoah Valley. In May 1862, at Front Royal, the regiment had a "sharp fight"

French-born Colonel Alfred N. Duffie led the First Rhode Island Cavalry.

against members of the Twelfth Georgia. They captured more than one hundred prisoners and recaptured twenty Federals, for a loss of ten killed and wounded.

During July 1862, the regiment camped in northern Virginia, where it received a new commander in the form of Colonel Alfred Duffie. A Frenchman, Duffie claimed to have been a graduate of the French military academy and a captain in the French army. In reality, while he had been awarded several medals and a battlefield commission for actions on the Crimea, he had deserted the French army and followed an American nurse back to New York City. Seeking military glory in a new country, he joined the First New York Cavalry in 1861. Sprague, looking for a competent military leader for the First Cavalry, selected Duffie. Every officer in the regiment resigned over the appointment, but the colonel, who spoke broken English in a comical manor, soon won them over, as he organized and disciplined the command.

A month later, at the Battle of Cedar Mountain, the First opened up the battle, taking heavy casualties while acting as skirmishers for the Federal line. The First Rhode Island was also unique in its first chaplain, Frederic Denison, a Baptist minister from Westerly. A member of the "church militant," he rode to war wearing a military uniform, a saber and a "seven barreled revolver." Always in the thick of the action, he later transferred to the Third Rhode Island Heavy Artillery and became a leading historian of the era after the war.

# The Cavalry

The First Rhode Island fought several more engagements in the fall of 1862 in the Shenandoah Valley before being heavily engaged at Kelly's Ford on March 17, 1863. Chaplain Denison recorded:

*Here the Regiment displayed great gallantry and achieved an honorable distinction. It charged across the river, the fords of which were deep, well defended and barricaded, repulsed the enemy, and took twenty-five prisoners. In crossing the river, Lieutenant Simeon A. Brown with eighteen men took the advance, and drove the rebels from their rifle pits. The 4th New York Cavalry had made two unsuccessful charges before Lieutenant Brown led forward his eighteen men. On the opposite bank one hundred rebels sheltered in earth works rained a deadly fire on the ford; on this side was a barricade so built that only one horse could leap over it at a time. Of the nineteen gallant soldiers who rode to the ford, only Lieutenant Simeon Brown, Sergeant Enos D. Guild, privates John A. Medbury and Patrick Parker reached the opposite bank, the other fifteen men were stopped by bullets striking them or their horses. The main body of the Regiment under Major Farrington promptly moved across the ford in support of Lieutenant Brown's forlorn hope, and the rebels fled from the rifle pits towards their horses, but twenty-five were captured by the 1st Rhode Island before they could mount. The river at the ford was four feet deep, the current very swift and some of the best rebel cavalry made a desperate defense. Three bullets pierced Lieutenant Brown's uniform and two wounded his horse, and the brave officer, after the battle, was summoned to the headquarters of General Hooker, who in person complimented Lieutenant Brown and recommended his promotion to the rank of captain. Colonel Duffie, in crossing at the head of the Regiment, had his horse wounded and fall under him. In an open field across the river three charges were made by the Union forces, each time driving the enemy. In this fight, the accomplished Assistant Adjutant-General of the Brigade, Lieutenant Nathaniel Bowditch, received a mortal wound. Major Farrington, Captains Allen Baker, Charles H. Thayer, and Augustus H. Bixby, Lieutenants George H. Thompson, George W. Easterbrooks, and George W. Darling, Sergeant James E. Bennett, and Corporal James W. Vincent, were among the wounded. Captain Thayer and Lieutenant Darling and fourteen enlisted men were taken prisoners. Lieutenant Henry L. Nicolai, a promising officer, and Sergeant Jeremiah Fitzgerald, were killed. The whole number of killed and wounded was twenty-six, and sixteen were taken prisoners, having charged too far into the enemy's lines.*

For his actions at Kelly's Ford, Colonel Duffie was promoted to brigadier general in June 1863.

The worst day of the war for the First Rhode Island Cavalry was June 17, 1863, at Middleburg, Virginia. Assigned to scout ahead of the main Union line, Duffie's orders were to billet his men in the town for the night. As a Frenchman, Duffie followed his orders explicitly. That night, his men rode into town and surprised J.E.B. Stuart, almost capturing the Rebel cavalry commander. Several hours later, Stuart returned with two brigades as the Rhode Islanders put up a desperate fight to hold their ground. Pressed on three sides, they eventually fell back, but Duffie decided to rest his men in a clump of trees that night instead of retreating. After the battle, the First Rhode Island tried to flee the next morning, but many of the horses were exhausted and more than two hundred men were captured by the enemy. Captain George N. Bliss bitterly wrote, "It is too bad to slaughter a regiment needlessly as we were. I may be egotistical, but I believe that if I had been in command I would have safely extricated the regiment from its perilous condition. I would have gone to a house, taken a man and told him to take me across the Bull Run Mountains and if he brought me amongst the Rebs I would have blown his brains out. We were halted all night when we ought to have been marching." One soldier recorded, "Our regiment has just been cleaned up." Duffie and most of his officers managed to escape; they were assigned to Washington, where they created a remount camp to rebuild the shattered command.

Throughout the rest of 1863, the First rebuilt its ranks and performed reconnaissance duty in northern Virginia. In June 1864, the regiment was transferred to the Petersburg area but was quickly recalled into the Shenandoah Valley. At Waynesboro, Captain George N. Bliss was awarded the Medal of Honor for leading a charge despite receiving three wounds. Throughout the fall of 1864, the First Rhode Island fought daily skirmishes with Confederate cavalry in the region. In one instance, General Duffie was captured by Mosby's Rangers.

Returning to Petersburg in January 1865, the regiment was consolidated into a battalion of four companies. Leaving in April 1865, the unit played a pivotal and leading role in the Appomattox Campaign, fighting at Five Forks and firing some of the last shots of the war at Appomattox Station on April 8, 1865. The men helped parole Confederate prisoners and retuned to Rhode Island in August 1865. According to regimental records, the unit was involved in more than sixty fights and skirmishes.

*Battle Honors: Front Royal, Cedar Mountain, Groveton, Second Bull Run, Chantilly, Fredericksburg, Kelly's Ford, Brandy Station, Middleburg, Deep Bottom, Opequon, Fisher's Hill, Cedar Creek, Luray, Mount Jackson, Waynesboro, Five Forks and Appomattox.*

# Second Rhode Island Cavalry

If there was one regiment that brought dishonor to the state of Rhode Island during the Civil War, it was the misunderstood Second Rhode Island Cavalry. The regiment was recruited in the fall of 1862 after the choicest men in the state had been recruited for the Seventh Rhode Island, Battery H, and the Second Battalion of the Fifth Rhode Island. Needing to fill up the regiment, the state authorized large bounties and sent recruiting agents to New York to find men—most of them were immigrants or criminals and quickly deserted.

Augustus W. Corliss of Providence, who had just returned from a three-month stint with the Seventh Squadron of Cavalry, commanded the unit. Many of the enlisted men in the Second were recent immigrants and could not speak English. Assigned to the Department of the Gulf, the Second Cavalry soon found itself engaged in hit-and-run battles with Confederate guerillas. The regiment participated in several minor engagements around Baton Rouge and took part in the Port Hudson Campaign. Fighting in the swamps of Louisiana took its toll on the regiment; few perished in combat, but the disease encountered in the bayous and the constant desertion of the immigrant-soldiers reduced the regiment well below the minimum standards. Few members of the Second took pride in the soldiering trade, allowing their weapons to rust, their horses to die of starvation and their clothing reduced to rags.

With fewer than two hundred men in ranks, General Nathaniel Banks decided to order the regiment consolidated with the First Louisiana Cavalry, a regiment raised among Louisiana loyalists fighting against the Confederacy. Consolidating regiments was not uncommon during the Civil War; indeed, several Rhode Island units were combined during the war. However, the consolidation of regiments from different states was unheard of. A member of the regiment wrote what happened next:

Major Augustus W. Corliss
commanded the Second and Seventh
Rhode Island Cavalries.

*The union of the Regiment with the First Louisiana Cavalry took place
September 1, 1863, contrary to the wishes of both officers and enlisted
men. Unwilling to lose their Rhode Island identity, they remonstrated
against a measure which the rank and file particularly regarded as arbitrary
and unjust. Some days before the consolidation occurred, they resolved that
when called upon to join the Louisiana regiment they would lay down their
arms rather than obey. Accordingly, when on the morning of September 1st,
Lieutenant-Colonel Robinson of the 1st Louisiana sent an order for the
Second Rhode Island Cavalry to transfer their camp to his; no one moved.
Learning the posture of affairs, he immediately rode over and repeated
the order in person, but the men simply replied, "We belong to Rhode
Island, and not to Louisiana." In fifteen minutes, the First Louisiana was
ordered up on foot, armed with sabres, revolvers and carbines, and formed
on the front and right of the Rhode Island Regiment. Lieutenant Colonel
Robinson then repeated the command previously given, adding the threat,
"Hurry up, or I will fire into you." Things now assumed a serious aspect.
The men saw that resistance would be useless, and with military law
against them, slowly fell into line. Their tardy movements excited the ire of
the Louisiana commander, and a file of men was ordered to lead Richard*

*Smith and William Davis, the two last to follow, to a field in front of the camp, where with their hands tied behind them, their eyes blinded, and without semblance of law, or form of trial, they were shot by two squads of men detailed from the Louisiana regiment. Davis fell killed. Smith was shot through the legs, and was afterwards dispatched by the revolvers of the Adjutant and Sergeant in charge. Lieutenant-Colonel Robinson then addressed the Rhode Island Cavalry in threatening terms, after which they marched back to camp filled with horror and indignation by the butchery they had witnessed. No candid person will say that the exigencies of the service authorized this severity, and the deed will live in history to shadow the memory of the officer by whose authority it was done.*

Governor Smith was outraged by what happened and demanded a full accounting from the War Department. A court of inquiry was launched into the actions of General Banks and Colonel Robinson, but no officers were ever brought up on charges.

After being forced from his regiment, Lieutenant Colonel Corliss joined the Regular Army, serving thirty years on the plains and in the Spanish-American War; he retired as a brigadier general. The men who survived their transfer to the Louisiana Cavalry were always bitter about the arrangement. In January 1864, the men of the Second, consolidated into two troops, were again joined, this time with the Third Rhode Island Cavalry.

*Battle Honors: Port Hudson.*

# THIRD RHODE ISLAND CAVALRY

The last white regiment raised in Rhode Island was the Third Rhode Island Cavalry, enlisted in the summer of 1863, consisting mostly of men who joined for the high bounty rather than a love of the cause. Recruitment went slowly, as the men, many of them underage, trained at a camp on Conanicut Island. In January 1864, the First Battalion left Rhode Island for Louisiana, where it was united with the two companies of the Second Rhode Island Cavalry.

The First Battalion immediately joined the advance up the Red River, where General Banks's forces were thrown back in haste when the gunboats supporting the mission became stuck in the mud and the Rebels attacked.

The Red River Campaign was the only major combat in which the Third was involved, and sparingly even then. Lieutenant Colonel Charles Parkhurst summarized what the Third did for the remainder of the war:

> *For the remainder of the term of service of the regiment their duties were only quasi military, as the conditions of affairs in Louisiana was only quasi civil, if indeed it has ever been more than quasi civil. The forces remaining in Louisiana were practically an armed force occupying the territory and trying to support and maintain the system of civil government which General Banks had endeavored to establish in the early part of 1864. Our chief duties were hunting guerillas and jayhawkers, and in protecting northern men who had leased the abandoned plantations and who were trying to make their fortunes in using the labor of the freedmen.*

The regiment remained on duty, but like the vast majority of Rhode Island regiments stationed outside the Army of the Potomac, they lost far more men to disease than to enemy fire, with the swamps of the Deep South producing a long list of regimental fatalities. The regiment spent the remainder of 1865 on picket duty in Louisiana. Finally, on November 27, 1865, the Third Rhode Island Cavalry, the last regiment raised by Rhode Island, became the last Rhode Island regiment mustered out of the service.

*Battle Honors: Red River.*

# SEVENTH SQUADRON, RHODE ISLAND CAVALRY

The Seventh Squadron of Rhode Island Cavalry is one of Rhode Island's more famous Civil War units, not so much for what the regiment accomplished during the three-month term of service but rather for the composition of the command. Company A of the regiment came from Providence. Company B, however, was composed of the students of Norwich University and Dartmouth College, earning the Seventh the moniker of the "College Cavaliers." The squadron was the brainchild of Sanford S. Burr, a student at Dartmouth, who felt that a three-month campaign would be a good break from the rigors of a classical education, while the men could also pursue glory to claim in their latter years. After being turned down by the governors

Francis Ewens joined the Seventh Rhode Island Cavalry in June 1862. He reenlisted in the Second Rhode Island Cavalry and died of disease in Louisiana.

of the other New England states, the idea of a college cavalry company was accepted by Governor Sprague. Together with a company hastily assembled in Providence, the battalion was assigned to duty in the Shenandoah Valley.

As one of the few cavalry units in the area, the small force of 175 men was always on guard. In one instance, two men were taken prisoner. In August, the regiment's only fatality, Arthur W. Coombs of Thetford, Vermont, a cadet at Norwich University, died of dysentery. The battalion evacuated Winchester with the rest of the Federal garrison in late August, moving into Harpers Ferry. Only days later, Stonewall Jackson and a large Confederate force began a siege of the garrison. Surrounded on all sides, the cavalry was given permission to attempt a breakout. Before the advance, Major Corliss warned his men that by morning they "would either be in Pennsylvania, in Richmond, or in hell." Private George S. Dewey of Hartford, Vermont, a junior at Dartmouth, wrote about the advance:

*Greencastle Penna*
*Sept. 16th 1862*

*Dear Friends,*

*You will doubtless be surprised to hear that we are in the free states but here we are but how long we are to stay no one knows. I wrote you from Harpers Ferry some ten days since but perhaps you did not receive it as all mail communications was cut off. I have it to a man who was going to try to get some dispatches through thinking that there might be a chance of your getting it. We were completely hemmed in at HF and last Saturday morning our pickets were driven off Maryland Heights and the battle commenced. It was pretty lively time for a while. About 7 oclock AM we were ordered across the river. It was some pretty hard fighting all the Am and part of the PM but at last the Rebels were too much for our men and finally drove them off from the mountain entirely, Our loss in killed and wounded was somewhere near 200. Our artillery kept putting the shells over amongst them all the PM and the AM on Sunday. About 1 oclock Sunday we were somewhat surprised by a shell passing just over our heads and bursting not 5 rods from where I was sitting. Then commenced the artillery duel. The rebels had two batterys planted on the mountains. Nothing was heard all the PM but the booming of the guns the whizzing of the shells! It was rumoured in camp that we were short of supplies and I am inclined to think that it was so. About 3 oclock Majr Corliss told us that the cavalry had permission from Genl. White to get out if we could About 9 in the eve some 2,000 of us started expecting a very bloody time.*

*One man was shot while crossing the bridge this we supposed was only a for taste of what was to come but very few shots were fired until we came near Hagerstown when we were startled by heavy firing in the advance. We drew pistols and dashed on to see what was up when we came up on a knoll we saw one Regt of our boys drawn up in line of battle in front of a rebel camp. This however was only a ruse but how the game was played I don't understand but I know it was a pretty shrewd thing for we not only passed by and through 20,000 of the enemy but also captured a baggage train consisting of 90 wagons and 63 prisoners and so it is said scared another train so badly they burned the train. You may be assured it was a dashing operation.*

*I have got to go and get my horse shod right now. So shall have to close and will tell the rest when I get home.*

*Yours in Haste*
*Will*

*You may get another letter from me in a week and you may not hear from me until I get home so don't worry about me.*

The Seventh Squadron successfully made it to Greencastle, Pennsylvania, before returning to Maryland to join the Army of the Potomac at Antietam, but it was not called on to fight. The squadron returned to Providence on September 26, and the students returned to their studies. After they graduated, many returned to the service. A proud boasting point in their postwar lives was service in the Seventh Squadron. Many of these men became lawyers, politicians, ministers and doctors. Zeeb Gilman, a Dartmouth man who served as a sergeant in the squadron, moved to California after the war and became a doctor. When he died in 1944, he was the last survivor to have served in a Rhode Island Civil War regiment.

*Battle Honors: Harpers Ferry.*

# Chapter 4

# The Light Artillery

## FIRST RHODE ISLAND BATTERY

Even before the Civil War, the Providence Marine Corps of Artillery had a proud history. Formed in 1802 to protect Providence shipping interests from pirates, the unit served in coastal defense during the War of 1812 and participated in the Dorr Rebellion. In the late 1840s, it became the first unit outside the Regular Army to operate horse-drawn artillery, serving as a model for units from Massachusetts and Connecticut. Throughout the late 1850s, the corps, under the command of Colonel William Sprague, later elected governor, drilled frequently for war.

When Sprague issued the call for arms, the marines were ready. Quickly raising their unit to full strength in three days, the unit, as the First Rhode Island Battery under the command of Captain Charles H. Tompkins, left Rhode Island on the morning of April 18, 1861. In the postwar years, it claimed to be the first group of Northern militia to leave for the front. Tompkins's men stayed for two weeks in Easton, Pennsylvania, where they received James rifles, becoming the first battery in the history of the United States Army to be equipped with rifled cannons. Joining the First Rhode Island Detached Militia at Camp Sprague, the battery then proceeded to reinforce a large Union force in the lower Shenandoah Valley. The only

William B. Rhodes of Warwick lost a brother who served in the navy and fought in every major battle of the war.

battle the battery participated in was a skirmish near Bunker Hill, Virginia, on the morning of July 15, 1861, briefly shelling the Confederate line.

After the skirmish, the battery remained in the Harpers Ferry area until relieved, lasting until the end of July, when it returned to Providence. With three months' service behind them, many of the men reenlisted or provided training to men joining other units.

*Battle Honors: None.*

# FIRST RHODE ISLAND LIGHT ARTILLERY REGIMENT

Rhode Island was unique among the New England states to raise and equip a full eight-battery regiment of light artillery; most states independently raised the small, 150-man batteries, providing no higher support or promotion potential for the officers. Because of the small size, the batteries could be quickly mobilized and sent to the front, with one per month recruited in the period of April–December 1861. The regiment was led by Colonel Charles H. Tompkins, a Providence merchant who commanded the Providence Marine Corps of Artillery before the war. The corps became known as "Mother of the Batteries." Tompkins was a gifted artillerist who trained his men hard and had the organizational insight to lead larger units. Lieutenant Colonel William Reynolds, another member of the corps, oversaw recruiting in Rhode Island before he was replaced by John Albert Munroe, who established a training camp in Washington for artillery recruits to learn the trade. Munroe wrote, "No arm of the service calls for greater intelligence, capacity, and judgment than the light artillery." He was correct, as cannoneers had to perform a multitude of tasks under fire, with men often working several positions on a gun crew at the same time.

Because a light artillery regiment was divided into battalions and batteries, the regiment never served as a complete unit; rather, the eight individual batteries were parceled out as needed. This wide range of distribution led one veteran to call the First Rhode Island Light Artillery the "Geography Class." Indeed, in July 1863, Batteries A, B, C, E and G were serving with the Army of the Potomac at Gettysburg, Battery D was on duty in Kentucky, Battery F served in North Carolina and Battery H was on duty in northern Virginia. All batteries benefited from the training provided by prewar members of the Providence Marine Corps

Major General Silas Casey of North Kingstown wrote the tactics manual used by the U.S. Army.

of Artillery. Because the regiment was a large organization, by the end of the war, most of the commissioned officers were men who had risen from the ranks and proven themselves as leaders under fire.

Although he did not have a regiment to command in the field, Colonel Tompkins and his other officers were busy with staff paperwork, while several of the officers rose to command artillery brigades in the Army of the Potomac; at Gettysburg, three out of seven infantry corps brigades were commanded by Rhode Islanders. Colonel Tompkins was wounded in the hand at Cedar Creek trying to save a gun of Battery G from capture. For his actions there, and on many other fields, he received the brevet or honorary rank of brigadier general for his services. Tompkins was replaced by Colonel John Gideon Hazard, who had entered the service as a lieutenant and likewise rose to the rank of brevet brigadier general. The First Rhode Island Light Artillery was the most famous unit Rhode Island sent to the war; indeed, afterward the veterans were proud to quip that the generals would not begin a battle until a Rhode Island battery was on the field.

Because the First Rhode Island Light Artillery never served as a regiment, but rather by battery, the history of each will be given here.

## *Battery A, First Rhode Island Light Artillery*

After Tompkins's Battery left in April 1861, a large contingent of men remained at the Benefit Street Arsenal. In May, these soldiers formed themselves as the Second Rhode Island Battery, later designated as Battery A, First Rhode Island Light Artillery. Accompanying the Second Rhode Island Volunteers to Camp Sprague, the soldiers learned firsthand the dangers of army life. A caisson containing ammunition exploded in camp, killing two and wounding three. The battery followed Burnside's Brigade to Bull Run, firing the first artillery rounds of the battle at Confederates on Henry House Hill. When their ammunition was expended, the battery retired with the loss of three dead and several wounded. The six guns of the battery were lost when the Cub Run Bridge was congested with wagons and spectators from Washington. Only one piece was recovered, by Private Charles V. Scott, who was eventually promoted to lieutenant for his actions. Today, the cannon, known as the "Bull Run Gun," is displayed at the Rhode Island Statehouse.

After Bull Run, the battery was sent to garrison the upper Potomac River and eventually became part of the Second Corps, Army of the Potomac. Captain John Tompkins, the brother of the regimental commander, ably commanded the unit throughout 1862. Fighting on the Peninsula, Battery A was heavily engaged at Fair Oaks, Savage's Station and Malvern Hill. On September 17, 1862, the unit was heavily engaged at Antietam. Fighting near the Dunker Church, the unit was constantly engaged in the morning fighting, firing more than one thousand rounds of ammunition, rendering its six cannons unfit for further service. Corporal Benjamin H. Child was struck in the head by a piece of shell but stayed by his cannon. For his actions, he was later awarded the Medal of Honor. Four soldiers died, while another fifteen were wounded. One of the most famous images of Antietam is that of a destroyed Confederate battery, with dead men and horses lying around an abandoned gun limber. Reviewing the destruction after the battle, Lieutenant Elisha Hunt Rhodes of the Second Rhode Island wrote, "It is said Battery A, Rhode Island Artillery did this work." For his actions, Tompkins was promoted to major and joined his brother Charles on the regimental staff. He was replaced by William Arnold, promoted from lieutenant in Battery E. In time, the unit became known as Arnold's Battery.

Engaged at Fredericksburg and Chancellorsville, Battery A's next major engagement was Gettysburg, where the cannoneers were in the center of the storm on July 3, 1863. Driver Thomas Aldrich recalled, "Without a moment's warning the heavens had opened, and the Union soldiers found themselves in a pitiless storm of shot and shell which burst and tore up the ground in all directions, dealing out death and destruction on every side." In the bombardment proceeding Pickett's Charge, the cannoneers helped

*Above:* Peter Hunt of East Providence was a lieutenant in Battery A and died at Cold Harbor.

*Left:* Private Joseph Lawrence of Battery A was killed at Antietam.

to shell the Confederate line. Five men were killed at Gettysburg. After the war, the veterans returned to Cemetery Ridge and dedicated a monument to their fallen comrades.

Joining the advance across the Rapidan in the spring of 1864, the battery participated at the Wilderness, Spotsylvania and Cold Harbor. Unfortunately, the unit also had the distinction of losing the first cannon the Second Corps ever lost to the enemy when it became stuck in a tree. On June 6, 1864, Battery A was mustered out of the service and returned home. Nearly fifty men who had reenlisted were assigned to Battery B, in which they fought until the end of the war.

*Battle Honors: Bull Run, Bolivar Heights, York Town, Fair Oaks, Savage Station, White Oak Swamp, Glendale, Malvern Hill, Chantilly, Antietam, Fredericksburg, Chancellorsville, Gettysburg, Bristoe Station, Mine Run, Wilderness, Po River, Spotsylvania, North Anna, Totopotomoy and Cold Harbor.*

## *Battery B, First Rhode Island Light Artillery*

Battery B was recruited in a span of three weeks in late July and early August. Most of the unit was recruited in Providence, but a sizeable contingent came from Exeter and West Greenwich. Assigned to the same brigade as Battery A, the men of Battery B were involved in the debacle known as Ball's Bluff in October 1861. Dragging a cannon across the Potomac River, the piece was lost to the enemy, while two men were killed and several more wounded as they attempted to flee from danger. The battery's first captain, Thomas Fales Vaughn, resigned shortly afterward and was replaced by Walter O. Bartlett, who was later forced from the army when it was discovered that he kept a prostitute in his tent. In August 1862, John G. Hazard was commissioned captain and placed in command.

Proceeding to the Peninsula, the unit was engaged at Fair Oaks and Malvern Hill. Held in reserve at Antietam, Battery B was thrown into the fury of Fredericksburg on December 13, 1862. With the Union infantry losing heavily, General Darius Couch needed to send a battery of guns to support his troops. Battery B was selected because it was equipped with smoothbore Napoleons, considered excellent guns for close-range work. As the soldiers galloped into action, their brothers in Battery A shouted out, "There goes Battery B to Hell!" Placing his guns just 150 yards from the entrenched Confederate line, Captain Hazard and his officers tried to dislodge the Rebels, but they would not move. With three men dead, fifteen wounded and a number of horses disabled, Hazard withdrew, but the sight was an inspiration to all who witnessed it, allowing the infantry to hold on to their position. General Couch complimented the men of Battery B, writing, "Men never fought more gallantly."

After Fredericksburg, Captain Hazard was appointed to brigade command and replaced by Lieutenant T. Fred Brown; soon, the unit was known as Brown's Battery B. The unit was lightly engaged in May 1863 at Marye's Heights. The supreme moment in the history of Battery B came at Gettysburg on July 2 and 3, 1863. On the afternoon of July 2, the battery was placed in an exposed position in Codori's Field to help protect the corps skirmish line. All of a sudden, a brigade of Georgians appeared. Turning his guns around to engage the enemy, Lieutenant Brown was shot in the neck, but he later recovered. Rhode Island cannoneers were constantly shot down as they tried to work the guns. With the help of some Pennsylvanians, four pieces were saved, but two were captured and later recaptured by the Nineteenth Maine. The next day, there were only enough men to work four cannons. In the bombardment of Cemetery Ridge before Pickett's Charge, the number four gun of the battery was hit by a shell, killing two men. When Sergeant Albert Straight and the surviving men tried to load the piece, the round became stuck in the muzzle, rendering the cannon inoperable. Taken to the rear, the cannon became one of the first relics of the war, and today it is on display at the Rhode Island Satehouse as the "Gettysburg Gun."

The battery next fought at Bristoe Station in October. During the Battle of Spotsylvania Court House, Battery B accomplished a remarkable feat. Much as the men did at Fredericksburg, supporting the infantry, a section of the command was brought into action in the Confederate trenches, blasting canister into the faces of the Rebels as they fought near the Mule Shoe Salient at Spotsylvania Court House. The battery followed the army to Petersburg, where they engaged in a daily struggle of life and death in the trenches. On August 25, 1864, at Ream's Station, the battery was overrun by a large force of Confederate infantry. Nearly fifty men and the four guns were captured, leaving a skeleton force to rebuild the shattered command.

Filled with recruits and the transferred veterans from Battery A, Battery B rose from the ashes, continuing to serve at Petersburg. The command was the first Second Corps battery on the road at Appomattox when the Confederate flag of surrender passed it on April 9, 1865. After the war, the veterans of Battery B dedicated two monuments at Gettysburg and wrote a regimental history to commemorate their deeds. Charles Tillinghast Straight, the son of

The Bull Run Gun of Battery A was saved from capture at Bull Run and is now on display at the Rhode Island Statehouse.

Sergeant Albert Straight, was an active member and became Rhode Island's leading Civil War historian at the turn of the twentieth century. The last battery veteran died in 1936.

*Battle Honors: Ball's Bluff, Yorktown, Fair Oaks, Malvern Hill, Antietam, First Fredericksburg, Second Fredericksburg, Gettysburg, Bristoe Station, Mine Run, Wilderness, Po River, Spotsylvania, North Anna, Totopotomoy, Cold Harbor, Petersburg, Deep Bottom, Ream's Station and Appomattox.*

## Battery C, First Rhode Island Light Artillery

The third battery to leave Rhode Island was Battery C, leaving in early September 1861. Like the previous two units, the battery drew heavily from Providence but included contingents from Pawtucket and Hope Valley as well. Among the members of the command was Edwin M. Stone of Providence. A correspondent for the *Providence Journal*, he sent home weekly letters about life in camp and the field. In 1864, these letters were collected and published as *Rhode Island in the Rebellion*.

Assigned to duty in Washington, the soldiers drilled hard under their captain, William B. Weeden, later a famous Rhode Island historian. The battery was assigned to the Fifth Corps and moved to the Virginia Peninsula. At the Siege of Yorktown in early April 1862, Private James Reynolds of Richmond had the unlucky distinction of becoming the first member of the Army of the Potomac killed in action on the Peninsula. The battery joined in the advance up the Peninsula and later took part in the Seven Days Battles. The bloodiest day of the war for Battery C was June 27, 1862, at Gaines Mill. Captain Weeden wrote of his men's participation in the battle as they fought the Texas Brigade:

> On the 27th it fought at Gaines' Farm with a vigor and bravery that commanded admiration. But courage and skill could not withstand the superior numbers hurled against the right wing of the Federal army, and after repelling repeated charges, the Battery was compelled to retire, losing severely in men and horses. Lieutenant Buckley, whose section was in position at the edge of the woods on General Martindale's right, had his horse shot. Three guns and three caissons were also lost: one being mired and abandoned and the others left on the field for want of horses to bring them off. During the battle, the colors of a rebel regiment were struck to the ground by a case shot from one of the guns of Lieutenant Buckley's section, and were never raised again. After he retired, they were brought in by the Second Maine regiment. Leaving this field of honorable disaster, the Battery proceeded by Charles City Cross Roads to Turkey Bend on the James river, and July 1st engaged in the bloody battle of Malvern Hill.

Six men died and nearly two dozen were wounded. Three days later, at Malvern Hill, a shell fired from a U.S. Navy gunboat accidentally hit the battery, killing another five men.

Two months later, at Second Bull Run, two caissons were abandoned on the field while the unit was held in reserve at Antietam. Two days later, however, they were heavily engaged in the rear-guard action at Shepherdstown, expanding more than five hundred rounds. One man was lost at Fredericksburg, where the battery helped cover the bridge-building activities of a group of Federal engineers. Battery C was heavily engaged at Chancellorsville, fighting alongside Battery A for two days against a determined foe and losing two more men to enemy fire. One member of the command remembered it as "fierce and bloody." Assigned to the Sixth Corps, the battery was held in reserve at Gettysburg but joined in the pursuit of Lee's army afterward; fifteen horses died of exhaustion by the side of the road.

Engaged again at Mine Run, the men spent a quiet winter at Brandy Station before joining their corps during the Overland Campaign. Except for being lightly engaged at Cold Harbor, the men of Battery C were held in reserve. Transferred to the Shenandoah Valley in July 1864, the battery again saw action at Cool Spring and then chased after the Rebel force. A sergeant remembered, "For several weeks we were in constant motion." Combat was finally joined again at Opequon in September, followed by Fisher's Hill three days later. On October 19, 1864, at Cedar Creek, Battery C was overrun by the Confederate army, losing two of its cannons and two comrades to the enemy. The guns were later recaptured.

After Cedar Creek, the battery, severely reduced in numbers, was sent to Washington. Lieutenant Jacob Lamb desperately tried to find recruits for his command but in the end was forced to consolidate his command with Battery G. The men of Battery C suffered the fourth-highest loss of a battery in the Civil War. Those who remained with Battery G fought until the end of the war.

*Battle Honors: Yorktown, Hanover Court House, Mechanicsville, Gaines Mill, Malvern Hill, Second Bull Run, Antietam, Fredericksburg, Chancellorsville, Gettysburg, Rappahannock Station, Mine Run, Wilderness, Spotsylvania, Cold Harbor, Petersburg, Opequon, Fisher's Hill and Cedar Creek.*

## Battery D, First Rhode Island Light Artillery

Battery D was unique among the Rhode Island batteries, as it was recruited entirely from Kent County. The unit was originally commanded by Captain John Albert Munroe of Providence, who had distinguished himself at Bull Run. Originally sent to join the First Corps, the battery spent the first year of its service drilling and performing guard duty near Fredericksburg. Munroe was a master tactician and drilled his men to quickly load and fire their cannons.

Battery D was first engaged at Groveton on August 27, 1862, losing a caisson and several wounded. Two days later, at Second Bull Run, the battery was under a constant fire, suffering three dead, as Captain Munroe and his officers each had a horse shot out from under them. Three weeks later, at Antietam, Battery D suffered heavy losses when it entered the fray early in the morning. Assigned a position near the Dunker Church, Private George C. Sumner recalled:

Private Joseph Corey of Battery D served from Scituate.

# The Light Artillery

*The minie bullets were beginning to come again, not so thick as before, but with a great deal of accuracy, and we soon found, that although we had driven the main line back, in the meantime quite a number of sharpshooters had dropped into the depression on the east side of the pike, and also behind a pile of rails on our right not over seventy-five yards away, and were making it very uncomfortable for us. The right piece of the centre section had three number ones shot down before they could load their piece, and had lost every man but Corp. Gray and Private Mills. The piece was finally loaded, and a shell was sent into the pile of rails, which must have done some damage. The right piece had lost every horse on its limber, and the other pieces were suffering losses in men and horses. It was no apparent that it was time for us to fall back if we wanted to save our battery.*

Among the wounded was Jeremiah Hopkins of the rural hamlet of Hopkins Hollow. Hit in the arm, Hopkins refused an amputation; he survived the wound and lived to be 101. Nine men died and sixteen were wounded, and thirty horses died. For his heroism at Antietam, Munroe was promoted to major.

Battery D was lightly engaged at Fredericksburg and then was transferred to Newport News with the Ninth Corps in February 1863. From here, Captain William Buckley took his men to Kentucky. On August 16, the battery began a long and tiring march with the corps into east Tennessee, a hotbed of unionism in the Southern state. Their mission was to protect the local populace from enemy attack. The march across the Cumberland Plateau was exhausting on horses and men, as they marched over 230 miles. In mid-November, the battery was stationed at Fort Saunders at Knoxville, Tennessee, when it was attacked by a heavy Confederate force. The battery's guns fired double charges of canister at the advancing enemy, playing a key role in driving them back. Cut off in an isolated location, Captain Buckley wrote about the condition of his men:

*The night of December 4th, the enemy evacuated their positions, after having besieged us for eighteen days. A great many of my horses were turned in unserviceable, as I could not get forage for them. The men were reduced to a small ration of beef and 1–8 of a loaf of bread per day, having no coffee, sugar or small rations. Many days were passed, however, when even this ration was omitted, and the men would be obliged to divide the few ears of corn left for the starving horses, among themselves, parch and eat it, to satisfy in a measure, the cravings of their empty stomachs.*

The men spent the winter of 1864 camped at Knoxville, which one veteran compared to Valley Forge. They did take part in a rare winter battle at Campbell's Station, Tennessee, suffering four wounded. In May 1864, the battery returned to the east with the Ninth Corps but was largely held in reserve until ordered to Washington as a surplus unit. Battery D was again assigned to the front that fall, taking part in the Shenandoah Valley Campaign as part of the Nineteenth Corps. The battery was overrun at Cedar Creek, losing most of its equipment and all of the battery record books. Elmer Corthell of Battery G was promoted to command for distinguished conduct at Cedar Creek. Battery D remained in the Shenandoah Valley, performing garrison duty at Winchester until it was mustered out in July 1865 and returned to Rhode Island.

*Battle Honors: Groveton, Second Bull Run, Antietam, Campaign of East Tennessee, Knoxville, Campbell's Station, Opequon, Fisher's Hill and Cedar Creek.*

## Battery E, First Rhode Island Light Artillery

Like Battery D before it, the majority of the soldiers in Battery E were recruited from the western towns of Foster, Scituate, Coventry and Cranston. Originally commanded by Captain George E. Randolph, his name was forever attached to the command. The command left Rhode Island in October 1861 and was assigned to the Third Corps. Private George Lewis of Coventry remembered an interesting story about a comrade: "Corporal Hale was reduced to the ranks for drunkenness and pugilistic conduct. He was not a Rhode Island, but joined the battery soon after our arrival in Washington. He was a man of some capacity, but had an unusual amount of self-conceit, and when intoxicated, he had, in his own estimation, few superiors."

With their command, the battery moved to the Peninsula in the spring of 1862, taking part in the battles at Yorktown, Glendale and Malvern Hill. At Glendale, Lieutenant Pardon S. Jastram threw his section into line, sending shot and shell into the advancing Confederate line, but soon he was forced back as they struggled to save their pieces from capture. With the horses dead in the traces, the gunners had no choice but to leave the pieces to the enemy, but they were later recaptured. Lieutenant Jastram was brought before a court-martial for not trying harder to save his guns but was later found not

Charles V. Scott saved the Bull Run Gun in the first major battle of the war, rose to brevet captain and died at Cedar Creek trying to save another gun.

guilty. At Malvern Hill, the battery engaged in long-range counter-battery fire with Confederate gunners. Among those wounded was Henry Binns, who had enlisted at age fourteen. Following Malvern Hill, the battery retired to Harrison's Landing. Rather than enemy fire, it was the dysentery, malaria and typhoid contracted there that took a toll on the command; many of the men from western Rhode Island had no immunity to disease, with nearly a dozen perishing before the command finally marched north in August 1862.

Battery E then fought at Second Bull Run, supporting the advance of Kearney's Division. Captain Randolph later wrote, "Battery E never fought better than in this action." Two men were killed and three were wounded in the fierce counter-battery action. For their heroism there, four men were awarded the Kearney Medal, a special Third Corps decoration. Detailed to Washington during the Antietam Campaign, the battery then fought at Fredericksburg in December 1862. Captain Randolph was promoted to command the Third Corps Artillery Brigade, as his battery fought in the desperate action south of town against Stonewall Jackson's Corps. As he drove his team into battle, Private Cornelius Sullivan shouted out, "The shot is not yet cast that will killed me!" Seconds later, a piece of case shot exploded overhead, tearing into his head and killing him instantly. Another soldier was killed, as well, and three were wounded. While the battery was engaged across the river, Private Edwin Matteson died of typhoid. Two

Lieutenant Colonel Percy Daniels
of Woonsocket served in the
Seventh Rhode Island.

of his brothers served in Battery B. Three days after the battle, George R. Matteson went to visit his brother "and was shocked to learn that his brother was dead and buried."

The battery received a number of recruits over the winter, but the majority of them deserted. The command joined the advance to Chancellorsville in May 1863, now commanded by First Lieutenant John Knight Bucklyn of Foster. A Brown graduate, he had enlisted as a private and worked his way up the ranks. On the evening of May 2, as the Confederates advanced up the Orange Turnpike, Bucklyn performed a heroic feat. Keeping his guns in action as the enemy approached, he continued to fire bursts of canister into their ranks. Bucklyn did not order his men to fall back, dragging their cannons back by prolong when the Rebels were twenty-five yards away. For his actions at Chancellorsville, Lieutenant Bucklyn was awarded the Medal of Honor; after the war, he became a principal in Mystic, Connecticut.

Battery E was again in the center of action on July 2, 1863, at Gettysburg. Sent out as part of the Third Corps advance, the unit was stationed on the Emmittsburg Road. That evening, the unit was hit by a brigade of Mississippians. Heavily engaged, Bucklyn and his men, with the help of the 114th Pennsylvania, tried in vain to hold the enemy back. The lieutenant was shot in the chest, believed to be a mortal wound. Six soldiers were killed and a further twenty wounded; half of the battery horses also died. Captain Randolph, commanding the Third Corps Artillery Brigade, was wounded in the fight as well, but the guns were saved from capture.

The unit fought at Mine Run in the fall of 1863 before being reassigned to the Sixth Corps, where like most of the Union army's artillery it played a minor role in the Overland Campaign of 1864. Assigned to garrison the trenches of Petersburg when the rest of the corps went to the Shenandoah Valley in the fall of 1864, the battery was assigned to "Fort Hell," where it engaged in a daily counter-battery struggle with the Confederates on the opposite side of the entrenchments. On the morning of April 2, 1865, Battery E fired the signal shot that was the sign for the Sixth Corps to assault the Confederate entrenchments. Assigned to guard captured Confederate artillery, the battery missed the Appomattox Campaign. It returned to Providence in June 1865 for muster out.

*Battle Honors: Yorktown, Charles City Cross Roads, Malvern Hill, Second Bull Run, Chantilly, Fredericksburg, Chancellorsville, Gettysburg, Mine Run, Wilderness, Spotsylvania, Cold Harbor and Petersburg.*

## *Battery F, First Rhode Island Light Artillery*

Battery F was unique among the eight batteries of the regiment. It was recruited in October 1861, largely from the mill villages of the Blackstone Valley and from Bristol and Newport Counties. Unlike the other batteries of the regiment, Battery F was originally commanded by Captain James F. Belger, who unlike his fellow commanders was not a member of the Providence Marine Corps of Artillery. Belger had served fifteen years in the Regular Army as a sergeant and was stationed at Fort Adams. Belger brought his men to Annapolis, Maryland, where they joined the Burnside Expedition.

Assigned to land on the coast of North Carolina, the battery did not make it to shore in time to participate in the Battle of New Berne. When the horses were being unloaded from the ship they were on, the animals were thrown into the sea and guided ashore by the call of the bugle they were used to hearing. Battery F became the only battery in the regiment to conduct an amphibious assault during the Civil War, something the original Providence Marine Corps of Artillery had been raised to accomplish. Because Burnside

Corporal Henry Nye of South
Kingstown served in Battery F.

did not have any cavalry with him, the battery put the cannons in reserve, mounting their horses and patrolling the roads leading to the city, losing several men in the process.

Throughout the summer of 1862, Battery F participated in parades and garrison duty at New Berne. In early December, the battery participated in a reconnaissance in force toward Goldsboro. In a fierce action on December 16, two men and twelve horses were killed, while the first sergeant lost his hand. Private Ethan Pendleton wrote of the expedition and of the news that he had just become a father: "We had 3 hard battles one at Kingston and 1 at White hall and 1 at Dudleys Mills ower los was 2 kild and 3 wounded James gavvit was kild he is George gavvits sun to Westerly. I was rather disapinded when I hurd that your baby was a girl you wanted to right a name I dont no that I can thinck of any I had rather that you name hur yoer self but if I should name hur I should call her Agnes." Battery F returned to New Berne, where it remained throughout the winter of 1863. On April 9, during an

Lieutenant Phillip S. Chase
commanded Battery F in 1864.

expedition to Blount's Creek, North Carolina, Captain Belger was severely wounded, leaving the command to Thomas Simpson.

In the spring of 1864, Battery F finally arrived in Virginia as part of the Eighteenth Corps. It was the first time that many of the other officers and soldiers of the First Rhode Island Light Artillery had seen their comrades in Battery F, leading to many welcome greetings from home. At Drewry's Bluff on May 14, two cannons and four limbers were captured by the Confederates, while two men and thirty-five horses were killed. Throughout the rest of the summer of 1864, the battery was constantly engaged at Bermuda Hundred, Chapin's Farm and other points north of Richmond in support of the Eighteenth Corps. Captain Simpson was captured by the enemy while returning to headquarters, as the original men were mustered out at the end of October. To take their place, a hasty recruiting drive was organized in Rhode Island to prevent the battery from being consolidated. Among the new recruits was Moses Orrin Knight of Scituate, whose brother, Alfred, had died in the service.

The battery remained encamped before Richmond during the spring of 1865, until the men marched into the city to perform garrison duty. Mustered out on June 27, 1865, Battery F returned to Rhode Island. According to Captain Simpson, "This Battery occupies a conspicuous place in the history of Rhode Island in the war."

*Battle Honors: New Berne, Fort Macon, Little Creek, Kinston, Whitehall, Rawle's Mill, Washington (North Carolina), Blount's Creek, Bermuda Hundred, Drewry's Bluff, Proctor's Creek and Petersburg.*

## *Battery G, First Rhode Island Light Artillery*

Battery G was the last organized unit Rhode Island sent to war in 1861. Two sections of the battery were raised in Providence, while a large contingent came from the southwestern communities of Charlestown, Hopkinton, Richmond and Westerly. James Barber was typical of the Battery G recruits. Twenty years old, he had lived in Westerly all his life and had been a fisherman before joining the army. Untypical was battery clerk George Lee Gaskell, a native of Sterling, Connecticut, who had recently returned from a voyage to the coast of east Africa and could speak French, Swahili, Arabic and Latin with ease. Both men left their mark on the unit.

Battery G's first captain was Charles D. Owen, at only nineteen one of the youngest commanders in the army. Owen was a member of the Providence Marine Corps of Artillery and had distinguished himself at Bull Run. The battery spent the winter of 1862 garrisoning the upper Potomac River. It was moved to the Virginia Peninsula in the spring of 1862 and took part in the Battle of Yorktown. Moving forward with the army, the unit was then

Private Albert D. Cordner enlisted in Battery G and later moved to North Dakota.

engaged at Fair Oaks on June 1. To bring the guns to the battlefield, Captain Owen had to lead them through a swamp; men and horses spent nearly eighteen hours trying to push the cannons five miles to the front. For the next month, Battery G remained encamped on the Fair Oaks battlefield. According to Private Gaskell, the only water to drink was tainted with blood from the battlefield, while the "death swamp" of the Chickahominy River proved fatal to many Battery G soldiers who came down with typhoid and dysentery. The battery fought at Malvern Hill during the Seven Days and then joined in the retreat off the Peninsula in late August.

Battery G joined in the pursuit of Lee's army into Maryland, taking a leading role at the Battle of Antietam. The unit was first engaged in the early morning fight near Dunker Church, shelling the Confederate line, as Lieutenant Otto Torslow, a Swedish officer serving with the battery, attempted in vain to rally the shattered Union line. Battery G then galloped into action near the Sunken Road, later known as Bloody Lane, to support the Union advance. Private Barber recalled, "Our Battery went galloping on to the disputed field riding on the dead both Union and Rebels as they lay on the field together." George Gaskell, carrying the battery guidon, recalled, "Shell flew above, balls around and beneath me." The battery engaged with a Confederate unit about a mile away, suffering five wounded before being relieved.

Battery G then supported the Union advance on Fredericksburg in December, shelling the city on December 11 and supporting the retreat on December 14–15, with the loss of one man. Captain Owen resigned his commission that winter and was replaced by Captain George W. Adams of Providence. At thirty, Adams was a gruff, no-nonsense combat veteran who trained his soldiers hard but was both loved and respected by his men. In time, Battery G became known simply as Adams' Battery. Adams arrived at a critical moment, as only twelve hours later the unit was engaged at the Battle of Marye's Heights in the Chancellorsville Campaign. Sent out to decoy the Confederates as the Sixth Corps formed up to take the hill, the unit came under a severe crossfire from Confederate cannons on Marye's Heights. Bugler William Lewis gave up playing his instrument and joined his fellow soldiers on a cannon: "I worked on the pieces the rest of the day but never had death stare me in the face so as it did. 4 men was shot down on the piece i was on i expected my turn to come next." Battery G was eventually pulled back a complete wreck, losing seven dead and twenty wounded. In addition, a caisson and gun carriage were also destroyed.

Following Chancellorsville, Battery G marched to Gettysburg but played no part in the main battle. Rather, on the night of July 5, at Fairfield, Pennsylvania, it helped to drive the last Confederate forces out of Pennsylvania through "a vigorous application of shot and shell." After emerging from winter camp, Battery G marched south with the Army of the Potomac in the spring of 1865. Held in reserve at the Wilderness, it fought for nearly eighteen hours without relief at Spotsylvania Court House on May 12, using hundreds of rounds. Again engaged at Cold Harbor, Adams had his men literally shell the tree line to eradicate Confederate snipers.

The command then moved to Petersburg before moving into the Shenandoah Valley, fighting at Cool Spring, Opequon and Fisher's Hill. On the morning of October 19, 1864, at Cedar Creek, the battery was caught in a surprise Confederate attack. Colonel Tompkins ordered the unit to hold its ground at all cost, sacrificing themselves to the enemy in order to buy precious time for the Union army to re-form. Bugler William Henry Lewis of Providence died trying to save a gun from capture. In total, nine cannoneers died and thirty more were wounded, but they managed to hold the line just long enough for the Vermont Brigade to form up and hold the line. Colonel Tompkins wrote, "The conduct of officers and men was gallant in the extreme and merits the hardy commendation of all who witnessed it. Rhode Island has just cause to be proud of such men."

Returning to Petersburg in January 1865, Captain Adams had one more plan for his command. On the morning of April 2, 1865, when the Sixth Corps assaulted the Confederate line, a small party of his men accompanied the Vermonters in their charge. Capturing two Confederate cannons, the cannoneers turned the guns around and began using them against their former owners. One soldier remembered it as "the most perilous exploit of the war." For his actions, Captain Adams received two brevets, and seven of his men received the Medal of Honor, including former fisherman and now corporal James Barber. The battery returned to Providence in June 1865 and was mustered out.

*Battle Honors: Yorktown, Fair Oaks, Malvern Hill, Antietam, Fredericksburg, Marye's Heights, Gettysburg, Rappahannock Station, Wilderness, Spotsylvania, Cold Harbor, Petersburg, Opequon, Fisher's Hill, Cedar Creek, Storming of Petersburg and Sailor's Creek.*

## *Battery H, First Rhode Island Light Artillery*

The last Rhode Island battery raised was Battery H, which was the eighth and final unit mustered for the First Rhode Island Light Artillery Regiment. Recruiting for the battery was excruciatingly slow, as many recruits were forwarded to the field as replacements for casualties suffered on the Peninsula. Finally, in October 1862, Battery H was ready for war, ably led by Captain Jeffry Hazard, a brother of Captain John G. Hazard. The battery was initially assigned to the defenses of Washington but suffered heavily from desertion. Throughout the winter of 1863, Captain Hazard had no choice but to draft men from a Vermont unit to keep his ranks filled until new recruits arrived. When troops were pulled out of the defenses of Washington to reinforce the Army of the Potomac in June 1863, Hazard resigned when Battery H was not included in the units joining the field army.

Replacing Hazard was Captain Crawford Allen, son of a wealthy manufacturing family. In the spring of 1864, the men of Battery H finally had their chance to join the Army of the Potomac, but much to their disgust, the unit was held in reserve at the Wilderness and Spotsylvania before being returned to Washington as a surplus unit. Finally, in 1865, the unit was returned to the front, joining the Sixth Corps Artillery at Petersburg.

On the morning of April 2, 1865, Allen's Battery joined the Sixth Corps troops on the front line as they stormed Petersburg. Firing more than 650 rounds, the battery successfully held back a Confederate attack, with the loss of four killed and several wounded; it was the only major combat the unit saw. Four days later, at Sailor's Creek, Battery H had the honor of firing the last shots fired by the Sixth Corps Artillery Brigade in the Civil War. Two months later, it was returned to Rhode Island for muster out.

*Battle Honors: Petersburg and Sailor's Creek.*

# TENTH RHODE ISLAND BATTERY

The Tenth Rhode Island Battery was raised under the same call as the Ninth and Tenth Rhode Island Regiments to serve three months in the defenses of Washington in the summer of 1862. The battery was composed largely of men from the Providence Marine Corps of Artillery. Armed with six Napoleon cannons, the unit drilled constantly for action and suffered one death, Corporal James Flate, killed in a training accident, proving how dangerous the artillery service could be. The unit was returned to Rhode Island in late August 1862.

In the summer of 1863, when it was feared that the Confederate raider *Alabama* was off the New England coast, Governor James Smith again called out the Tenth Battery to serve as part of the defenses of Narragansett Bay. The unit erected a camp at "The Bonnet" in North Kingstown, helping to rebuild a Revolutionary-era fort. The men spent the summer on picket duty, occasionally firing at passing ships that did not fly the United States colors. Many men considered it a summer holiday rather than a military commitment and were disappointed when they were forced to return to Providence that fall and muster out.

*Battle Honors: None.*

# Chapter 5

# The Heavy Artillery

## THIRD RHODE ISLAND HEAVY ARTILLERY

The Third Rhode Island Heavy Artillery was the largest organization that Rhode Island sent to the field during the Civil War. Mustering more than two thousand men during the regiment's existence, the unit fought as light and heavy artillery, engineers, infantry and cavalry and even manned gunboats with the navy. The regiment fought battles in Virginia, South Carolina, Georgia and Florida. Hastily raised in the weeks after Bull Run to serve three years, the Third's companies drew from the following Rhode Island communities:

- Battery A: Providence
- Battery B: Providence
- Battery C: Providence
- Battery D: Pawtucket
- Battery E: Providence
- Battery F: Providence
- Battery G: Warwick
- Battery H: Providence
- Battery I: Providence

- Battery K: "Irish Company," recruited at large
- Battery L: Providence
- Battery M: Providence

Originally commanded by Colonel Nathaniel Brown, a veteran of the Rhode Island Militia, the regiment went into camp at Warwick before leaving in August for Long Island. Here they joined an expedition under the command of Brigadier General Thomas West Sherman of Newport, bound for the coast of South Carolina. Upon arrival in the southern theater of the war, many of the men experienced the cause they were fighting for as hundreds of escaped slaves sought refuge in the Union camp. Late in 1861, the regiment was converted to heavy artillery. Two additional companies were recruited, and the regiment was divided into three four-battery battalions, allowing it to be spread throughout the Department of the South.

In early April 1862, a battalion from the regiment was deployed to Savannah to lay siege to Confederate-held Fort Pulaski. A member of the regiment recalled:

*April 10th at 8:15 A.M., the bombardment opened from the mortar batteries, and by 9:30 all the heavy rifle guns were in full play. The mortar batteries proved a grievous failure, as less than one tenth of the 1512 shells thrown by them fell inside the fort, and it became evident before night that the breaching batteries alone must be depended upon to reduce the fort. All these were manned by the men of the Third Rhode Island, with the exception of Battery Sigel, equipped with light pieces, 5 thirty-pounder Parrotts and 1 forty-eight pounder James rifle, which were not served with efficiency during the first day. The bombardment was kept up until evening, and the wall of the fort was fast becoming honey-combed. One mortar and one 30-pound Parrott continued the fire all night, to prevent repairs, and at sunrise on the 11th all the batteries opened again with decided effect, until the breach in the wall exposed the magazine and rendered longer resistance dangerous. The firing from both the rifle guns and Columbiads was excellent, "the former boring like augers into the brick face of the wall, the latter striking like trip-hammers and breaking off great masses of masonry that had been cut loose by the rifles." At 2 P.M. the fort surrendered, 385 men, including a full complement of officers, several severely, and one mortally wounded. On the Union side one man only was killed, Thomas Campbell of Co. H. Sergt. George W. Greene, of Co. B, was wounded in the face. None of*

*Above*: Lieutenant Erastus Bartholomew, Third Rhode Island Heavy Artillery, of Woonsocket, fell at Secessionville.

*Right*: Captain Peter Turner of Newport served in the Third Rhode Island Heavy Artillery.

*our guns were hit. The most effective batteries were those served by the Rhode Island men, and in particular, the battery of James rifles manned by Co. H, which threw 570 shot and 225 shell. The battery manned by Co. F threw 441 shot, and the one manned by Co. B threw 749 shells. The heavy James rifles of Battery McClellan, under Capt. Rogers, ably seconded by Lieutenants Charles R. Brayton and William C. Barney, were the most effective instruments in reducing the fort, as acknowledged by Gen. Gilmore in his report. The service of these guns, bearing the name of a distinguished Rhode Islander, wrought in this siege a revolution in the use of siege guns. Says Gen. Gilmore: "Had we possessed our present knowledge of their power previous to the bombardment of Fort Pulaski, the eight weeks of laborious preparation for its reduction could have been curtailed to one week, as heavy mortars and Columbiads would have been omitted from the armament of the batteries as unsuitable for breaching at long ranges."*

Fort Pulaski was the first battle for the regiment and proved the usefulness of long-range artillery fire. It also marked the end of the usefulness of brick-and-mortar seacoast fortifications, which could now easily be destroyed by rifled artillery fire.

In June 1862, five companies of the Third acting as infantry, accompanied by another battery equipped as a light artillery unit, advanced against Charleston, South Carolina. Bogged down in a swamp, the Rhode Islanders lost heavily at the Battle of Secessionville on June 16. Trying to hold their ground, the Rhode Islanders eventually fell back when pressed by a superior Confederate force. In the fall of 1862, the unit participated in the Battle of Pocotaligo, landing a force of artillerymen from a naval vessel to operate a battery of boat howitzers in support of the infantry advance. In addition, that fall, Colonel Brown died of yellow fever, becoming the highest-ranking Rhode Island officer to die of disease in the Civil War. He was replaced by Colonel Edwin Metcalf, who in turn was replaced by Charles Brayton. After the war, Brayton became infamous as "Boss Brayton," running Rhode Island's Republican political machine for half a century.

Throughout the winter of 1863, the regiment was divided throughout South Carolina and the coast of Georgia. Companies A and C were detached to serve as light field batteries, while the remainder of the regiment began siege operations against Fort Sumter, using its heavy guns to pound the fort daily, but the defiant Rebels refused to yield. In June and July 1863, the Third began siege operations against Fort Wagner, working

Lieutenant Henry Pendleton of Hopkinton served in the Third Rhode Island Heavy Artillery.

with the Fifty-fourth Massachusetts in its operations. After the Confederate evacuation of Wagner in September 1863, the regiment continued to bombard Fort Sumter on a daily basis, as it was considered the symbol that started the Civil War.

During the spring of 1864, Battery A accompanied the failed expedition into Florida that resulted in the Battle of Olustee. Meanwhile, Battery C was sent to Virginia to join the Eighteenth Corps, fighting alongside the soldiers of Battery F, First Rhode Island Light Artillery. The remainder of the regiment remained in South Carolina and Florida, engaging enemy shipping and playing a supporting role in the Battle of Honey Hill that fall. Because the regiment never served together as a complete unit in the field, the various batteries were mustered out throughout the summer of 1865. In concluding a brief history of the Third Rhode Island Heavy Artillery, Chaplain Frederic Denison of Westerly noted, "Thus closed the services of the largest military organization ever sent into the field by the State of Rhode Island, and one whose term of service extended from August 14, 1861 to August 27, 1865."

*Battle Honors: Fort Pulaski, Secessionville, Pocotoligo, Laurel Hill, Fort Sumter, Fort Wagner, Fort Burnham, Deveaux Neck, Honey Hill, Olustee, Drury's Bluff and Petersburg.*

# FIFTH RHODE ISLAND HEAVY ARTILLERY

As with the Third Rhode Island Heavy Artillery before it, the Fifth Rhode Island Heavy Artillery began its term of service as an infantry regiment. The Fifth was initially raised as the "Burnside Battalion." The men enlisted with the promise of easy duty along the coast of North Carolina as part of the Burnside Expedition; few could have imagined that the recruiting promise would be broken even before the regiment saw combat. First commanded by Major John Wright, the unit originally had five companies, later joined by Companies F through K, recruited as follows:

- Company A: Providence
- Company B: Barrington, Bristol and Warren
- Company C: Providence
- Company D: Woonsocket
- Company E: Providence
- Company F: Providence
- Company G: Newport
- Company H: Newport
- Company I: Providence
- Company K: Providence

The regiment left Rhode Island in December 1861 and, together with Battery F and the Fourth Rhode Island, joined the Burnside Expedition at Annapolis.

The journey to North Carolina was rough on the regiment, as it was chronically short of food and water. Landing on Roanoke Island in February, the men garrisoned the island until the division was moved toward New Berne. The battle of March 14, 1862, proved to be the Fifth's only major combat. Charging alongside the Fourth Rhode Island, the five companies struggled to advance, constantly tripping over their long sword/bayonet scabbards. Among those killed was First Lieutenant Henry Peirce, the high school principal in Woonsocket. The lieutenant had "abandoned the profession of teaching from a sense of duty. In his short military career he proved himself a good soldier." At a cost of eight dead, the Fifth helped capture the city.

First Sergeant Daniel Dove served in the Fifth Rhode Island Heavy Artillery.

Following the Battle of New Berne, the Fifth participated in the Siege of Fort Macon, thus completing "a succession of honorable victories," as General Burnside called his campaign. Throughout the rest of 1862, the Fifth remained at New Berne, drilling and performing picket duty. Beginning in September, an additional five companies were recruited, primarily in Newport and Providence, to bring the regiment up to full strength; because of a large number of vacancies, many of the original members of the regiment became commissioned officers. Colonel Henry Sisson of Little Compton replaced Major Wright as the commander of the Fifth as well.

In December 1862, the regiment participated in a reconnaissance in force for the first time into the North Carolina interior. Lieutenant Colonel Job Arnold wrote of the engagement at Rawle's Mill:

> *At the commencement of the action, we received orders to support Belger's Rhode Island battery. We formed in line to the right and rear of the battery, in the cornfield to the right of the road. When the battery moved to take its position, we filed down the road and formed a line about twenty paces in the rear of the battery in the field to the left of the road, our right resting toward the road, and there remained till ordered to follow the battery across the ford. We had nearly reached the road when we were ordered to remain to support a section of Belger's battery, left in its former position. We then formed in line in rear of a rail fence to the left and rear of the pieces, our left resting on the woods. As soon as the battery was ordered forward we joined the main column, and, crossing the ford, proceeded with it up the road*

Nathan B. Lewis was a proud veteran of the Seventh Rhode Island.

*to the rifle pits this side of Rawle's Mill, and remained within supporting distance of the battery while it was engaged in shelling the enemy. At about one o'clock, we entered the rifle-pits, and there remained until daylight. At one time, the regiment was under quite heavy fire, and it gives me much pleasure to state that both officers and men, without exception, behaved with the most perfect coolness.*

The regiment also participated in the engagement at Goldsboro, losing one man killed and four wounded.

Recruiting posters such as this enticed Rhode Islanders to join the service.

In 1863, the Fifth became a heavy artillery regiment but did not raise the additional two companies needed to create a full regiment. Assigned to garrison a line of fortifications along the North Carolina coast, the regiment, much like the Third Rhode Island, was spread out and vulnerable. One of the worst incidents in the history of Rhode Island in the Civil War occurred on May 5, 1864, as the Battle of the Wilderness raged in Virginia. Captain William W. Douglass wrote:

*During several months in the early part of 1864, Company A had been stationed at Croatan, N.C. This place is situated on the line of the Atlantic and North Carolina Railroad, twelve miles south of New Berne, about half a mile east of Boyce's Creek, and six miles from Havelock, going south. Croatan is an isolated place, and exceedingly difficult of access except by railroad, and had been held since the capture of New Berne simply to prevent guerrillas from tearing up the railroad track and cutting the telegraph wires. About 7.30 o'clock on the morning of the 5th instant, the enemy appeared in considerable force at Croatan, having effected the crossing of Boyce's Creek at a point above our pickets. Arriving*

*Left*: Captain Levi Tower of Pawtucket died at Bull Run serving in the Second Rhode Island.

*Right*: Lieutenant Colonel Joseph B. Curtis, Fourth Rhode Island, fell at Fredericksburg.

*at the station they immediately surrounded the force stationed there in preparation for an attack, and to prevent the possibility of any escaping. In the meantime Captain Aigan collected his men and threw his entire command into the fort at that place, which had one small gun, a six-pounder howitzer, and opened a vigorous fire on the enemy. A desperate fight ensued, lasting one hour and a half, when, at 12 o'clock, M., the enemy demanded an unconditional surrender. This was refused by Captain Aigan. Subsequently, however, seeing he could maintain his position but a short time, and the ammunition for the field piece being exhausted, he agreed at 3 o'clock P.M., to a conditional surrender. The force brought against Captain Aigan, as stated to him by the rebel General Dearing, was at least 1600 men. During the fight 184 rounds were fired from the single cannon with which the fort was defended, and the rifles of the men became so hot that they had to be held by the slings. This determined defense excited the admiration even of the enemy, and drew from their General, remarks complimentary to the bravery of the Union commander. Fortunately, not one of Captain Aigan's command was killed and but one wounded. The loss of the enemy was not less than twenty killed and wounded. The rebels violated the terms of capitulation in every particular but one, and that was, that the little garrison should march out with the honors of war. This was done to the tune of "Yankee Doodle." The men and officers were afterwards shamefully robbed of their private property. Captain Aigan and Chaplain White (who had been on a visit to the post) were permitted at first to retain their swords, but in less than an hour they were taken away by General Dearing's order. The Chaplain found it difficult to retain his spurs and gauntlets, and his horse that had been shot in action was stripped of all the accoutrements, including the Chaplain's blanket, while officers high in rank insisted that Captain Aigan should give up his dress coat. The treatment of the prisoners on the march, and in the prisons at Kinston, Macon and Andersonville, was inhuman in the extreme. Of the fifty-one captured, thirty-two died in prison, seven died elsewhere, and one was shot in attempting to escape. Captain Aigan was taken to Charleston with other officers to be placed under fire, and was moved thence to Columbia, S.C.*

Among the men who died in prison were three sets of brothers. After the war, a monument to the state's prisoners of war was erected at Andersonville in honor of the Rhode Islanders who perished there.

After the loss of Company A, the men remained on alert, but except for fighting a battle against yellow fever in which scores of the men died, the Civil War gradually shifted away from the coast of North Carolina. On June 26, 1865, the Fifth Rhode Island Heavy Artillery returned home. Greeting the regiment at the dock was Major General Ambrose Burnside, under whose name the battalion had first enlisted. Although consigned to the "backwater of the Rebellion," the men of the Fifth had answered the call with the usual ardor of Rhode Islanders and performed their duty. Veterans of the Fifth later returned to New Berne, together with those of the Fourth and Battery F, to dedicate a monument at New Berne National Cemetery in honor of the soldiers from the state who died in North Carolina. In 1890, the veterans successfully petitioned the state for funds to publish a regimental history, thus allowing the men of the state to share their story for posterity.

*Battle Honors: Roanoke Island, New Berne, Fort Macon, Kinston, Whitehall, Goldsboro, Rawle's Mill, Little Washington, First Rebel Attack on New Berne and Second Rebel Attack on New Berne.*

Governor James Y. Smith replaced William Sprague as Rhode Island's chief executive.

# FOURTEENTH RHODE ISLAND HEAVY ARTILLERY

Rhode Islanders were no strangers to slavery. In the eighteenth century, Newport had been one of the largest importers of African slaves, while large plantations staffed by slaves were spread throughout South County. At one point, nearly 10 percent of the state was black. By the mid-nineteenth century, Rhode Island's blacks had settled into the background, with small populations in Newport, South County and Providence. Here they worked the jobs others did not want, as barbers, gardeners and laborers. Racial tension had always been present between whites and blacks in Providence, with several bloody riots in the early part of the nineteenth century.

In September 1862, Governor Sprague issued calls for Rhode Island to recruit a black regiment, the first raised in the North. Rallying to the cry of Rhode Island's First Regiment, a unit of freed slaves that had fought in the Revolution, nearly one hundred men enrolled. Unfortunately, the unit was never activated, as it was feared that they would be assigned as laborers instead of combat soldiers. By the summer of 1863, such fears had subsided as black units distinguished themselves at Fort Wagner and Milliken's Bend. In July, Governor Smith requested activation of one company of heavy artillery to staff the defenses of Narragansett Bay. The call went out, and within days, the full complement of 150 men had been recruited from Providence and South County. Shortly after, Smith received orders to activate a four-company battalion and, finally, a full twelve-company regiment of heavy artillery.

The governor had no problem selecting officers for the regiment. In order to become an officer in the unit, the candidate had to have at least three months of prior service and pass the Casey Board, an officer review panel conducted by Major General Silas Casey of North Kingstown. Many of the officers were combat veterans who could not gain a commission in their own regiment because of a lack of vacancies. By joining the Fourteenth, they not only received a commission but also brought combat experience with them to train their men. The problem facing Smith was that a full regiment of heavy artillery was nearly 1,800 men. Rhode Island's small black population could only support enough soldiers to outfit Companies A and B. The rest of the unit was recruited mostly from New York, Ohio, Kentucky and Tennessee. Here the state appointed recruiters to find suitable men to enlist. Many of these state-sponsored agents, who were not military officers, swindled the men they recruited out of their bounty money by

Captain Joshua M. Addeman was a native of New Zealand who came to Rhode Island as a youth. He served in the Fourteenth Rhode Island Heavy Artillery and later became the second-longest-serving secretary of state.

making them pay for the trip to Rhode Island. Many of the soldiers were illiterate, with little education, and gladly paid the money for the chance to serve. Governor Smith launched an investigation, but little of the money was ever recovered.

The men were forwarded to a training camp on Dutch Island, where they trained until forwarded to New Orleans one battalion at a time. Each battalion received a flag from the governor that carried the word "Colored" in the regimental designation to set it apart from the white troops with whom they served. The First Battalion left in December 1863, going to Passo Cavallo, Texas, where it garrisoned Fort Esparanza. The battalion evacuated the fort in May 1864 as the First and Third Battalions were sent to perform garrison duty in New Orleans, while the Second Battalion was stationed at Camp Parapet, north of the city. The only combat the regiment saw was in May 1864, when three members of Company G who were on picket duty were captured and executed in cold blood. Lieutenant George Gaskell, promoted from Battery G, wrote about life in Plaquemine, Louisiana, to his sister back home in Connecticut:

# The Heavy Artillery

*Placquemine, La.*
*Aug. 28th, 1864*

*My Dear Sister*

*I have been waiting the past week in hopes of getting a mail. I know that two Steamers are in at New Orleans, but there is not one to send up our mail from there. So I may as well write at once or you may begun to think that I am "gone up" as we say. I am in better health the past week but my liver troubles me occasionally.*

*Of all the stout, hardy, fine looking officers that trod the deck of the "Dan Webster" on their way South. There is not now <u>one</u> who can be called <u>Sound</u>. All or more less sick, some very low. But don't you have the blues, Never fear for me. The people of Ct. have not got rid of me so easy as that. But tis difficult to get out of the service, sometimes I think of getting into home in the summer. Tis 5 years since I have been at home in this month (August). So habituated have I grown to the semi-civilized life I have known since then, enjoy life one month to be with you in Central Village. Could I not keep you busy learning stories of past activities and scenes.*

*What has become of the Greenvillers. I never hear from them or of them, neither of the Pawtucket people and to tell the truth I do not write to them myself. I tried to keep up a correspondence with Emily but she is too careless for a writer.*

*Esther Hall has written 4 or 5 times since I came out here. She seems to be a good kind of girl doesn't much over love our sex and from the specimens in and about Sterling I don't blame her. I wonder how Card prospers also Carrie Whitford—where does the later live and how. How are the Sherpards. Remember me to Reuben, Mr. French and Hannah.*

*We expect to get paid in a few weeks. I have owning me over 400 dollars and owe about half of it but when new are paid I shall send you some money.*

*Things are up slightly here. Cotton will be worth in a couple of weeks 2.00 dollars a pound. The crop is ruined by caterpillars. Sugar will go up steadily. I expect to see it 60 cents in a few weeks.*

*A pair of boots is worth here from 18 to 24 dolls, ladies shoes 6 to 11 and all things just outside our lines are doubled. I know plenty of ladies who carry out a dress pattern of common cheap print getting it through our lines under their hoop skirt and selling it for 40 or 60 dollars. Many a <u>lady</u> I have passed out wearing a new pair of shoes and noticed on returning she would perhaps have a pair of old slips, or perhaps nothing at all.*

*Oh Mary you can't conceive how these Southern women hate us with of course exceptions of a few who have it may be of interest to keep them on our side.*

*One of our duties is the picket at the two entrances to the town where the officers examine passes and searches the vehicles to see that no goods contraband to war are carried out. Every one taking out anything has to have a permit from the Provost Marshall stating the kind of goods and amount. Anything not embraced on the list has to be seized and confiscated.*

*You may well believe this a trying position for a young officer when some young lady comes along and has some little thing which she could not get a permit for. Then all her powers of persuasion comes up and if the officer gallantly overcomes his duty he generally gets (whats some satisfaction to us poor devils) is a sweet smile. But on the other hand if Duty carries the day and the goods are turned back you may believe that they don't spare their sneers. A couple days ago I was so ungallant as to make a very pretty woman get out of her carriage, ostensibly that I might search under the seats, but really to notice any unusual expansion about the hoops knowing that the lady in question had on occasion carried out several revolvers under her garments. This time however I was at fault and I got a pretty shower of abuse you may believe. About a dozen times she exclaimed "I thought you Yankees claimed to be gentlemen." To which I only bowed and answered "Madame I am a soldier. Je vous souhaite un bon matin." (I wish you a good morning) for she was a Creole. Such are the incidents occurring some dozen times a day. We have to be on duty every other day and night.*

*Our Regt. is now the 11th United States Heavy Artillery. For the present direct your letters as usual.*
*I will write to you when we get paid before I send you any money so you may be on the look out.*
*Now Sister Mary Don't fail to write often as possible.*

*And believe me to be (your)*

*Brother George*

*Can't you scare me up some pictures from home of anybody no matter who Excuse Postage*

Much to the disgust of the enlisted men, the regiment largely performed fatigue duty, being used as laborers to construct fortifications at Plaquemine and New Orleans. The soldiers established a camp newspaper, while the regimental officers established a school to teach the men the fundamentals of reading and writing. Several of the sergeants passed the Casey Board exam but, owing to prejudice, were not commissioned. In order to bring full recognition to state-raised black units, the Fourteenth lost its state designation when it was renamed the Eleventh United States Colored Heavy Artillery.

At Plaquemine, the soldiers of the Second Battalion had frequent contact with the local populace, inspecting their wagons to ensure that no contraband was smuggled through the lines. Because he spoke French, Lieutenant Gaskell became the provost martial of the district, being able to speak to the local Acadians. Gaskell eventually married into a French family and spent the rest of his life in the South. Although the soldiers of the Fourteenth never engaged in a battle, they trained hard and doubtless would have excelled under their veteran officers. Unfortunately, the fortunes of war relegated the regiment to the backwater of the war.

While they never engaged in combat, the Fourteenth fought a horrendous battle with disease. Nearly four hundred members of the regiment died of the terrible illness encountered in the Louisiana bayou country; this was the most suffered by any Rhode Island regiment. It fell to the lot of First Lieutenant William H. Chenery to write the history of his regiment, which became the Fourteenth's monument. In his concluding remarks, he could find no better memorial for the Fourteenth:

> *We may not boast the honor of inscribing on our banners long list of battles, yet may we not point with pardonable pride to services faithfully performed on the picket line, and in the daily routine of camp and garrison duty. Let the many mounds in the lowlands of Louisiana, where we laid away the silent forms of our comrades in the untimely graves to which they had been borne, through the deadly effects of miasmatic swamps, testify to our contribution of noble souls who freely gave their lives for the preservation of this republic, the blessings of which we and our descendents now fully enjoy.*

*Battle Honors: None.*

*Chapter 6*

# Aftermath

The 1860 census found 174,620 people living within the 1,200 square miles that compose Rhode Island. Of these, 35,502 were males between eighteen and forty-five, the military-age population. Rhode Island officially received credit for sending 23,236 men to war, a staggering 67 percent of the prewar military-age population. Many men outside this age bracket fought as well, with some soldiers as young as fourteen and others as old as sixty going to war. Fighting in nearly every major Civil War engagement, Rhode Island troops left indelible marks on the battlefields; 23 Rhode Islanders were awarded the Medal of Honor for heroism in action. When the last bugle sounded, more than 2,000 Rhode Islanders were dead in the crusade to free the slave and preserve the Union.

From the start, Rhode Islanders remembered their Civil War dead. Families of deceased soldiers paid, if they could, the $100 it took to bring a loved one's body back from the South. Even without the physical presence of their father, son or brother, many families spared no expense to erect a fitting memorial in their memory. Typical of these monuments was one erected in the Usquepaugh Village Cemetery. Private Charles Gardiner was a nineteen-year-old soldier who served in Company G, Seventh Rhode Island Volunteers. Gardiner survived Fredericksburg but, like so many of his comrades, contracted dysentery in Mississippi, and he died of the illness in Ohio. His remains were brought back to Rhode Island and interred in the soil of his native state. The inscription that his parents chose for his headstone indicates that this soldier was deeply cared for:

*Charles W. Gardiner*
*Son of Benjamin C. & Mary W. Gardiner*
*Died at U.S. Hospital,*
*Cincinnati, Ohio,*
*Aug. 24, 1863,*
*Aged 19 years, 11 mos.*
*& 18 days.*
*Member of Co. G 7th Reg. R.I. Volunteers*

*Time hath not the power to bear away,*
*Thine image from the heart*
*No scenes that mark lives onward way,*
*Can bid it hence depart.*

*Yet while our souls with anguish riven,*
*Mourn dearest one for thee*
*We raise our tearful eyes towards heaven,*
*When our dark path appears.*

*'Tis sweet to know, though canst not share*
*Our anguish and our tears*
*For though hast gained a brighter land,*
*And death's cold shroud is past.*

*Thine are the rays of God's bright hand*
*That shall forever last*
*Be strong on thy angel brow*
*Thy home is with the savior now.*

Still standing in South Kingstown, this memorial and hundreds more like it blight the cemeteries of Rhode Island, mute witnesses to the terrible suffering undertaken by the young men of Rhode Island.

In 1868, Rhode Island was one of the first states to create a post of the Grand Army of the Republic, the largest Union veterans organization. Prescott Post No. 1—named after Lieutenant Henry Prescott of the First Rhode Island who died at Bull Run and whose body was never recovered—organized at the Benefit Street Arsenal. By the end of the nineteenth century, twenty-seven posts were spread throughout Rhode

In 1908, the veterans of the Seventh Rhode Island dedicated this monument at Vicksburg, Mississippi.

Island. Meeting biweekly in their posts across the state, the men sought to remember their fallen comrades by traveling to their graves each May "to decorate them with the choicest flowers of spring." In 1872, Rhode Island became the first state to make Decoration Day, now Memorial Day, a state holiday. One veteran, Elisha Watson of Coventry, made a fifty-mile circuit through the Pawtuxet Valley every year until he was ninety-five.

Furthermore, the old soldiers recorded their memories for posterity through regimental histories. In 1890, the state allocated funds to purchase a history of every regiment and battery furnished by the state to the war; few regiments failed to comply. As such, Rhode Island has one of the richest collections of published memoirs of Northern states. In addition to this, the General Assembly authorized a monument for every Rhode Island unit. The granite quarries of Westerly were busy as well, building monuments to be placed on battlefields throughout the South, including *Old Simon*, a large statue of a Union soldier that stands guard over the Federal dead at Antietam. By the fiftieth anniversary of the Civil War, monuments for Rhode Islanders were erected at Andersonville, Gettysburg, New Berne and Vicksburg.

*Left*: The toll of battle: Alfred S. Knight of Scituate was one of the more than two thousand Rhode Islanders who died in the Civil War.

*Below*: After the war, the veterans of Wickford formed the Charles Baker Post of the Grand Army of the Republic.

# Aftermath

Veterans of Westerly pose during a Memorial Day ceremony at the turn of the twentieth century on the steps of their Grand Army of the Republic Hall in downtown Westerly; it is now the Westerly Public Library.

In 1875, the veterans of Rhode Island formed an organization called the Soldiers and Sailors Historical Society. Meeting monthly in Providence, the group was distinct from the Grand Army of the Republic in that it not only honored Union veterans but also sought to record Rhode Island's participation in the Civil War. The veterans collected letters and artifacts carried by Rhode Islanders and formed a large library, which they housed at the Providence Public Library. Beginning in 1878, the Soldiers and Sailors Historical Society began publishing a series of pamphlets titled Personal Narratives of the Battles of the Rebellion. Eventually reaching one hundred volumes, the booklets are invaluable resources about studying Rhode Island's role in the Civil War, providing firsthand accounts found nowhere else. The society met as late as 1915 before turning its collections over to the Providence Public Library, where the gathered treasures remained. Unfortunately, many of the items, including a photograph of the first Rhode

*Above*: Despite losing his arm at Spotsylvania Court House, James Hoard became chief of police in Bristol.

*Left*: Henry Joshua Spooner served as adjutant of the Fourth Rhode Island and served five terms in the House of Representatives.

Islander to die in the Civil War, the guidon of the Second Corps Artillery Brigade flown at Gettysburg and a sword of General Burnside, have been lost to the ravages of time.

In 1890, the Rhode Island General Assembly began to appropriate $200 to every regimental and battery organization from Rhode Island to publish a regimental history, a book about the unit's service in the Civil War. Ranging from a simple journal of occurrences, as is the case with the Battery D regimental history, to the massive text of narratives, biographical sketches and photographs that compose the history of the Seventh Rhode Island, nearly every Rhode Island regiment left behind a written record of its wartime service. Even 150 years later, these books are some of the best sources on the subject. The foresight of the General Assembly allowed the deeds of Rhode Island's Civil War veterans to not be forgotten. In 1893, the state also published a massive two-volume set, *Revised Register of Rhode Island Volunteers*, listing each soldier from Rhode Island who served in the war.

Many Rhode Island veterans returned to their homes and continued on with the same lives they led before the war. William O. Harrington served three years in Company K, Seventh Rhode Island, surviving Fredericksburg and the Mississippi Campaign, while his best friend was killed standing next to him at Cold Harbor. He returned to his farm in Foster, meeting a son born days after he left for the front; Harrington's brother, a doctor in the Eighteenth Connecticut, died in the war. Harrington joined the Grand Army of the Republic and died in 1904, proudly carving his wartime service on his headstone. James Hoard of Warren lost an arm at Spotsylvania, and he returned home to become chief of police in Bristol, while Daniel Hoxsie, who survived wounds at Chancellorsville, Cold Harbor and Cedar Creek, returned to Richmond and died in extreme poverty. James A. Barber of Westerly never let the fact that he was a Medal of Honor recipient get in the way of his daily life. He continued working as a fisherman and operated a lifesaving station at Watch Hill.

Many Rhode Island veterans used their wartime service as a springboard toward a successful career in business or politics during the war. Nathan B. Lewis of Exeter worked on his father's farm and taught school during the winter before he enlisted. Only rising to the rank of corporal, Lewis returned to Exeter and joined the postal service, quickly becoming postmaster. He studied law at night, joined the bar and eventually became a circuit judge in Washington County. Lewis was known as a fair and equitable practitioner and also served in the Rhode Island General Assembly. Active in veterans affairs, he never missed a

Colonel James Shaw of Providence led U.S. Colored Troops.

reunion and served as president of the Seventh Rhode Island Veterans Association from 1893 until his death in 1925.

Before the war, Edwin Allen was a clerk in Hopkinton. He rose from private to first lieutenant in the conflict, returned home and served thirty years as town clerk in Hopkinton and a term as lieutenant governor of Rhode Island. His brother, Edward, who shot himself in the foot by accident at Petersburg, moved to San Francisco and became active in politics as well. Henry Joshua Spooner of the Fourth Rhode Island served five terms in the House of Representatives, while Nelson Aldrich, a veteran of the Tenth Rhode Island, became the United States senator who introduced the amendment for a national income tax.

Despite his portrayal as a poor, incompetent commander, Ambrose Burnside proved to be Rhode Island's greatest Civil War hero. He returned to the state a hero, and in 1866, he was elected to the first of his three terms as governor. Among his accomplishments was arranging to have a memorial erected in Providence listing every soldier from Rhode Island who died in the conflict, as well as presenting a testimonial of service to every Rhode Island veteran. In 1871, he became the first president of the National Rifle Association, as well as the first Rhode Islander to become the national commander in chief of the Grand Army of the Republic. Elected to the United States Senate in 1874, he tried to modernize the U.S. Army.

Burnside was a soldier who always tried to do his duty, but because of a misinterpretation or deliberate neglect of his orders, he was considered a failure by many. Although Burnside died in 1881, Rhode Islanders honored his memory by placing an equestrian statue of him in Providence.

While Burnside's stature rose dramatically after the war, that of Governor William Sprague sunk tragically. Elected to the Senate in 1863, he attempted numerous times to acquire a field command but was rebuffed. In the Panic of 1873, he nearly lost his textile empire. While in a drunken tirade on the Senate floor, he called Rhode Island's Civil War soldiers "a craven band of misfits" and was replaced in the Senate by Burnside. Politically dead, he retired to his farm in Narragansett, but in a continuing series of bad luck, the farm was consumed by fire. Today, Canonchet Farm is home to the South County Museum and its marvelous collection. When Sprague died in 1915, the Providence Marine Corps of Artillery fired the parting salute.

By the turn of the century, nearly every Rhode Island community had dedicated a monument or a Grand Army Hall to honor its Civil War dead. Scituate was one of the last, erecting a memorial in honor of the forty men from the small town who died in the service. The names were familiar to many of the older men and women in town: Alfred Sheldon Knight, who died of pneumonia while serving in the Seventh Rhode Island; David B. King, shot in the head while working a cannon at Gettysburg with Battery B; Richard Edwin Taylor of the Seventh, who had survived so much only to die in the last charge of the war; Lewis Medbury, who fell at Chancellorsville; Thomas Tinkham, who died of disease; and Henry and John Lawton, brothers who had fought in the Second Rhode Island, one falling on the Peninsula and the other at Spotsylvania. During the dedication, Daniel Ballou, the state commander, went to the podium and delivered a fitting address about Rhode Island's contribution to the war. During a recent visit to the Rhode Island Statehouse, he had a flashback to his youth:

> *I have stood with uncovered head and looked upon the tattered and stained battle flags and guidons now safely sheltered within the walls of our lordly state capitol, a few of them at one time borne by the soldiers of R.I. in the battles of the Revolution, but most of them by R.I. boys in the great battles of the Civil War, and have fancied I could hear the tramp of marching columns, the din and clamor of battle, the hoarse cries of command, and see the colors borne by dauntless hands far in advance and*

*the men gallantly pressing forward amid the withering fire of hurtling shot and singing bullets, steadily lining up to them for a bloody struggle. It was but a momentary illusion, and my eyes rested again only on torn, stained and tattered flags.*

The monument still stands in the village of North Scituate today. Thousands of motorists pass it daily, few stopping to read the names inscribed on its base; meanwhile, on top, a lone sentinel stands waiting, gazing off at the horizon as if waiting for the boys of Scituate to come home.

The last Civil War veteran from Rhode Island was John Riley of Scituate. The son of Irish immigrants, his father died at Bull Run fighting with the Second Rhode Island Volunteers. Spending the majority of the war working in the mills of the Pawtuxet Valley, he joined up in March 1865, serving with Company H, Second Rhode Island Volunteers, when bounties were high and victory near certain. Fighting in the last battles of the Petersburg Campaign, Riley was mustered out in the summer of 1865, returning to a life of millwork in Scituate. Uninterested in veterans affairs, he did not join the Grand Army of the Republic until his nineties. Comrade John Riley died in 1943 at age 101 and was buried at Manchester Cemetery in Coventry, near many of his comrades, his stone being inscribed: "To the last man."

With the passing of the last veteran went the living connection Rhode Islanders had to the Great Rebellion. Today, only faded photographs and carefully preserved letters remain. However, in town centers and cemeteries, in libraries and archives throughout the smallest state, something remains, a physical reminder to those who seek it of the days when Rhode Islanders gladly offered themselves up for the causes of union and emancipation. The soldiers who served from Rhode Island left behind a record unsurpassed, serving in nearly every major battle of the conflict. They left their mark in the battle honors now inscribed on their disintegrating flags in the statehouse in Providence.

# Rhode Island Medal of Honor Recipients

The following is a listing of men, either native-born Rhode Islanders or those serving with Rhode Island units, who were awarded the Medal of Honor for heroism in the face of the enemy during the Civil War. It is drawn from the Medal of Honor files at the National Archives.

BABCOCK, WILLIAM J.
Rank and organization: Sergeant, Company E, 2nd Rhode Island Infantry
Place and date: Petersburg, Virginia, April 2, 1865
Date of issue: March 2, 1895
Citation: Planted the flag upon the parapet while the enemy still occupied the line; was the first of his regiment to enter the works.
Buried: Riverside Cemetery, Wakefield, Rhode Island

BARBER, JAMES A.
Rank and organization: Corporal, Battery G, 1st Rhode Island Light Artillery
Place and date: Petersburg, Virginia, April 2, 1865
Date of issue: June 20, 1866
Citation: Was one of a detachment of twenty picked artillerymen who voluntarily accompanied an infantry assaulting party, and who turned upon the enemy the guns captured in the assault.
Buried: Riverbend Cemetery, Westerly, Rhode Island

BLISS, GEORGE N.
Rank and organization: Captain, Company C, 1st Rhode Island Cavalry
Place and date: Waynesboro, Virginia, September 28, 1864
Date of issue: August 3, 1897
Citation: While in command of the provost guard in the village, he saw the Union lines returning before the attack of a greatly superior force of the enemy, mustered his guard, and, without orders, joined in the defense and charged the enemy without support. He received three saber wounds, his horse was shot, and he was taken prisoner.
Buried: Lakeside/Carpenter Cemetery, East Providence, Rhode Island

BLISS, ZENAS R.
Rank and organization: Colonel, 7th Rhode Island Infantry
Place and date: Fredericksburg, Virginia, December 13, 1862
Date of issue: December 30, 1898
Citation: This officer, to encourage his regiment; which had never before been in action, and which had been ordered to lie down to protect itself from the enemy's fire, arose to his feet, advanced in front of the line, and himself fired several shots at the enemy at short range, being fully exposed to their fire at the time.
Buried: Arlington National Cemetery, Arlington, Virginia

BUCKLYN, GEORGE N.
Rank and organization: First Lieutenant, Battery E, 1st Rhode Island Light Artillery
Place and date: Chancellorsville, Virginia, May 3, 1863
Date of issue: July 13, 1899
Citation: Though himself wounded, gallantly fought his section of the battery under a fierce fire from the enemy until his ammunition was all expended, many of the cannoneers and most of the horses killed or wounded, and the enemy within 25 yards of the guns, when, disabling one piece, he brought off the other in safety.
Buried: Fishtown Cemetery, Mystic, Connecticut

BURBANK, JAMES H.
Rank and organization: Sergeant, Company K, 4th Rhode Island Infantry
Place and date: Blackwater, near Franklin, Virginia, October 3, 1862
Date of issue: July 27, 1896

Citation: Gallantry in action while on detached service on board the gunboat *Barney.*
Buried: Miltonville, Kansas

CHILD, BENJAMIN H.
Rank and organization: Corporal, Battery A, 1st Rhode Island Light Artillery
Place and date: Antietam, Maryland, September 17, 1862
Date of issue: July 20, 1897
Citation: Was wounded and taken to the rear insensible, but when partially recovered insisted on returning to the battery and resumed command of his piece, so remaining until the close of the battle.
Buried: Swan Point Cemetery, Providence, Rhode Island

CORCORAN, JOHN
Rank and organization: Private, Battery G, 1st Rhode Island Light Artillery
Place and date: Petersburg, Virginia, April 2, 1865
Date of issue: November 2, 1887
Citation: Was one of a detachment of twenty picked artillerymen who voluntarily accompanied an infantry assaulting party, and who turned upon the enemy the guns captured in the assault.
Buried: Oak Grove Cemetery, Pawtucket, Rhode Island

EDWARDS, JOHN
Rank and organization: Captain of the Top, U.S. Navy
Citation: As second captain of a gun on board the USS *Lackawanna* during successful attacks against Fort Morgan, rebel gunboats and the ram *Tennessee* in Mobile Bay, on 5 August 1864. Wounded when an enemy shell struck, Edwards refused to go below for aid and, as heavy return fire continued to strike his vessel, took the place of the first captain and carried out his duties during the prolonged action which resulted in the capture of the prize ram *Tennessee* and in the damaging and destruction of batteries at Fort Morgan.
Buried: Pocasset Cemetery, Cranston, Rhode Island

ENNIS, CHARLES D.
Rank and organization: Private, Battery G, 1st Rhode Island Light Artillery
Place and date: Petersburg, Virginia, April 2, 1865
Date of issue: June 28, 1892

Citation: Was one of a detachment of twenty picked artillerymen who voluntarily accompanied an infantry assaulting party and who turned upon the enemy the guns captured in the assault.
Buried: White Brook Cemetery, Richmond, Rhode Island

HAVRON, JOHN H.
Rank and organization: Sergeant, Battery G, 1st Rhode Island Light Artillery
Place and date: Petersburg, Virginia, April 2, 1865
Date of issue: June 16, 1866
Citation: Was one of a detachment of twenty picked artillerymen who voluntarily accompanied an infantry assaulting party and who turned upon the enemy the guns captured in the assault.
Buried: New Orleans, Louisiana

HAYES, THOMAS
Rank and organization: Coxswain, U.S. Navy
Citation: As Captain of No. 1 gun on board the USS *Richmond* during action against rebel forts and gunboats and with the ram *Tennessee* in Mobile Bay, August 5, 1864. Cool and courageous at his station throughout the prolonged action, Hayes maintained fire from his gun on Fort Morgan and on ships of the Confederacy despite extremely heavy return fire.
Buried: Unknown

LEWIS, SAMUEL E.
Rank and organization: Corporal, Battery G, 1st Rhode Island Light Artillery
Place and date: Petersburg, Virginia, April 2, 1865
Date of issue: June 16, 1866
Citation: Was one of a detachment of twenty picked artillerymen who voluntarily accompanied an infantry assaulting party and who turned upon the enemy the guns captured in the assault.
Buried: North Burial Ground, Providence, Rhode Island

McDONALD, GEORGE E.
Born: Warwick, RI
Rank and organization: Private, Battery L, 1st Connecticut Heavy Artillery
Place and date: Fort Stedman, Virginia, March 25, 1865
Birth: Warwick, Rhode Island
Date of issue: July 21, 1865

Citation: Capture of flag.
Buried: Oak Grove Cemetery, Pawtucket, Rhode Island

MALBOURNE, ARCHIBALD
Rank and organization: Sergeant, Battery G, 1st Rhode Island Light Artillery
Place and date: Petersburg, Virginia, April 2, 1865
Date of issue: June 20, 1866
Citation: Was one of a detachment of twenty picked artillerymen who voluntarily accompanied an infantry assaulting party and who turned upon the enemy the guns captured in the assault.
Buried: Bennett and Gordon Lot, Field Hill Road, Scituate, Rhode Island

PARKER, THOMAS
Rank and organization: Corporal, Company B, 2nd Rhode Island Infantry
Place and date: Petersburg, Virginia, April 2, 1865, and Sailor's Creek, Virginia, April 6, 1865
Date of issue: May 29, 1867
Citation. Planted the first color on the enemy's works. Carried the regimental colors over the creek after the regiment had broken and been repulsed.
Buried: Memorial Cemetery, Philadelphia, Pennsylvania

POTTER, GEORGE W.
Rank and organization: Private, Battery G, 1st Rhode Island Light Artillery
Place and date: Petersburg, Virginia, April 2, 1865
Date of issue: March 4, 1886
Citation: Was one of a detachment of twenty picked artillerymen who voluntarily accompanied an infantry assaulting party, and who turned upon the enemy the guns captured in the assault.
Buried: Swan Point Cemetery, Providence, Rhode Island

READ, GEORGE E.
Rank and organization: Seaman, U.S. Navy
Date of issue: December 31, 1864
Citation: Served as seaman on board the USS *Kearsarge* when she destroyed the *Alabama* off Cherbourg, France, 19 June 1864. Acting as the first loader of the No. 2 gun during this bitter engagement, Read exhibited marked coolness and good conduct and was highly recommended for his gallantry under fire by his divisional officer.
Buried: Littleneck Cemetery, East Providence, Rhode Island

STEVENS, HAZARD
Born: Newport, RI
Rank and organization: Captain and Assistant Adjutant General, U.S. Volunteers
Place and Date: Fort Huger, Virginia, April 19, 1863
Date of issue: June 13, 1894
Citation: Gallantly led a party that assaulted and captured the fort.
Buried: Island Cemetery, Newport, Rhode Island

TAYLOR, JOSEPH
Rank and organization: Private, Company E, 7th Rhode Island Infantry
Place and date: Weldon Railroad, Virginia, August 18, 1864
Date of issue: July 20, 1897
Citation: While acting as an orderly to a general officer on the field and alone, encountered a picket of three of the enemy and compelled their surrender.
Buried: Greenwood Cemetery, Coventry, Rhode Island

WELSH, JAMES
Rank and organization: Private, Company E, 4th Rhode Island Infantry
Place and date: Petersburg, Virginia, July 30, 1864
Date of issue: June 3, 1895
Citation: Bore off the regimental colors after the color sergeant had been wounded and the color corporal bearing the colors killed thereby saving the colors from capture.
Buried: Blackstone, Massachusetts

# The Letters of
# Major Peleg E. Peckham

During the course of this author's research into the part played by Rhode Island in the Civil War, few letters had a more powerful message or impact than those written by a carpenter from Charlestown, Rhode Island. This man is Peleg E. Peckham. During his two and a half years of war, Peckham changed remarkably in his views. After his regiment had been annihilated at Fredericksburg in December 1862 and President Lincoln issued the Emancipation Proclamation, he hoped that a revolution would take place and remove Lincoln from office. He was a good soldier who believed that his cause was to restore the Union, not to free the slave. This viewpoint is clearly expressed in the first two letters. Peckham's experiences in the next two years of war changed all of this; the war finally turned in favor of U.S. forces. Before the 1864 presidential election, where the very fate of the United States was on the line, he wrote an impassioned letter to the *Providence Journal*, urging Rhode Islanders to vote for Lincoln. He knew that if the president was not reelected, all of the hard work that he and his thousands of fellow soldiers had accomplished would come to naught.

Peleg Edwin Peckham was born in the village of Shannock, Rhode Island, on April 6, 1835. Peleg was part of the sixth generation of Peckhams to settle in Rhode Island. His father, Rowland, was born in Westerly on June 20, 1791. Rowland married Mary Johnson of Westerly and had eight children. The Peckham family had a deeply rooted military tradition: his grandfather fought in the Revolution, his father in the War of 1812 and his brother, Edwin, in the Civil War as a member of Battery B, First Rhode

Hailing from Shannock, Brevet Major Peleg Edwin Peckham's view of President Abraham Lincoln changed dramatically during the war.

Island Artillery.[1] Peleg was educated in the local schools while learning carpentry. He was married in 1860 in New York City to Martha E. Ennis of Charlestown; they had one son, Frank, who would become a successful Providence doctor.

Peleg carried on his profession until August 1, 1862. On this day, he enlisted, with nearly one hundred other men from southwestern Rhode Island, as a private in Company A, Seventh Rhode Island Volunteers, but was quickly promoted to sergeant. After receiving its initial training around Washington, the Seventh fought at Fredericksburg on December 13, 1862.[2] During one stage of the battle, Peckham acted as a courier, delivering messages under fire. For his courage, he was awarded a battlefield promotion to second lieutenant; promotion to first lieutenant came in March 1863.[3] After the Mississippi Campaign in the summer of 1863, Peckham was one of only three remaining company officers fit enough to be on duty. After a tour on staff duty in Kentucky in late 1863 and the winter of 1864, he was transferred back to the Seventh as it moved to Virginia; here he assumed command of Company B.

During the bloody May 18 battle near Spotsylvania Court House, Lieutenant Peckham led his company into a desperate charge. He was rewarded with a regular promotion to captain in addition to a brevet of major. This was his last line battle, as he became a permanent staff officer.[4]

He returned home for two months of rest in November–December 1864 but was back at the front at Petersburg in January 1865. On April 2, 1865, General Ulysses S. Grant ordered a head-on assault against Petersburg. The mission was successful, and the Seventh only lost sixteen men. During a lull in the fighting, Peckham was eating lunch when he was suddenly caught in a crossfire and shot in the head. He was carried to the rear and only regained consciousness to tell the surgeon, "Tell my wife." Brevet Major Peleg E. Peckham died at 3:00 p.m. on April 2, 1865, at age twenty-nine. His remains were returned to Westerly and buried at River Bend Cemetery.[5]

The first two Peckham letters are in the author's private collection. The third was printed in the *Providence Journal* on November 7, 1864. All editorial notations were taken from William P. Hopkins's *The Seventh Regiment Rhode Island Volunteers in the Civil War: 1862–1865* and the *Revised Register of Rhode Island Volunteers*, vol. 1 (Providence, RI: E.L. Freeman, 1893). Note that as the letters were transcribed from the originals, the spelling and punctuation may prove difficult for a modern reader.

Letter I. After the disastrous Battle of Fredericksburg, during which the Seventh Rhode Island lost 220 men, it established a winter camp near Falmouth, Virginia. Here disease and privation ran rampant, supplies were low and the morale of the army was broken. On New Year's Day 1863, the Emancipation Proclamation announcing that all slaves held in territories rebelling against the United States would be "forever free" went into effect. This permanently changed the objective of the war—it was no longer just about preserving the Union but was about freeing the slaves as well. Many soldiers resented the change, including Peleg Peckham, who here writes to Captain David R. Kenyon of Richmond. Kenyon was a friend and neighbor of Peckham's who was recovering at home after being wounded at Fredericksburg.

*Camp of the 7th Regt RI Vols*
*near Falmouth, Va*
*January 4th 1863*

*Lt. D.R. Kenyon*
*Dear Friend*

*Yours of the 31st Dec is at hand received this evening and seize the earliest opportunity to answer it for I have not much else to do but to write, besides*

*I do not know why but all it is very lonesome here I do not know why but all in camp complaining of its being very lonesome that time drags heavily along. I am glad to learn that you arrived home safe. I presume you somewhat surprised the good people of Richmond when you arrived there I can imagine meeting as you hobbled into the presence of your wife. You write that political gossip is at an ebb there just now, well it will revive up soon but you surprise me that Governor Sprague[6] will be in the field again in the Spring but now is the poplar feeling toward him is it favorable or not in R. Island at any rate he dont attend to his business much for he had not sent along my commission yet nor attended to the promotions at all in this Regt. it went out on picket duty New Years with only five commissioned officers Col. Bliss is now a Brigadier General[7] had Nagles Brigade[8] Nagles commanding Sturgis Division Sturgis having been appointed to the command of the Defence of Washinton[9] Capt Carr[10] whose resignation had been withdrawn has now tendered it again with a view to its acceptance Lieut Inman[11] has resigned + gone home Leut Healys[12] resignation is going to the circuit and I heard last night that Lieut Hunt was about to resign and I shouldnt wonder if there were others that resigned if theirs accepted. Church is Acting Col[13] & Capt Tobay Major[14] Lieut Stone is on Bliss staff[15] and Lieut Robert if the 12th also.[16] We "the Pioneers" have been pitching tents the Head Qtrs. Tents and building the chimneys today. John D. Lewis[17] is dead we buried him beside Jerome Kenyon[18] it is currently rumored that another move will be made in immediately. We are all under marching orders with three days provisions in our haversacks & 5 to be in the wagons. Some think we are going back to Warrenton + thence to Culpepper to Gordonsville to Richmond but I am of opinion that we are going to Harrison Landing and up the Peninsular but I do not know as it makes much difference which way we go if we only get there. I presume you have read the President's last + quietly digested it. But not so with me it lays on my stomach like leaven Flour water cakes. It burns & paine killer is the only remedy for that So Democracy is the only Antidote against the permanent disunion of these States. I look upon that Proclomation[19] as the weakest of any of Uncle Abes productions in that line he in his philanthropic sympathy for the external nigger has left all the poor cusses still in bondage while he has declared others over whom he cannot now and probably never will gain any power free. I think if I had been in his place I would either declared all the Black rascals free or I would let them all entirely alone. I am satisfied that the last link is now broken that binds the North and the South togeather. The President had struck a blow that has cut the hearts of the Southern people to the quick. And then are firmly united in the defence of their rights and privileges under the Constituiton. As were our father of old in breaking the yoke of British tyranny Besides will the people of the North sustain the President as carrying out this as he says "War" I say dangerous Measure me think there will be a division of sentiment about that matter and unless our arms win the next great battle which I presume in not far distant are crowned with success depend upon it there will be a revolution at once & Old Abe will be hurled from his seat the Cabinet turned out the doors + that imbecile political family completely destroyed to give place to such men as Gov. Seymour of NY[20] & Arnold of our own little state & with little Mac[21] near then I think a peace might be conquered and this now destracted and by Republican rule almost ruined country would soon be restored to its once happy state of prosperity and standing as a nation and this black page of history be handed down to future generation as the evidence of the first triumph of the REPUBLICAN PARTY that of the near disoloution of this great nation & certainly is nearly financial ruin but I am no doubt getting tedious & I will close the boys have all been receiving boxes from home but my wife writes that the express man will not take the one she fitted up for me if you can bring my box do so if you cannot make the trip and make room for the boots in your trunk & bring them to me so good night & write me again on receipt of this how your leg gets along and when you will probably be back + oblige Your Obt. Servant Peleg Peckham*

Letter II. The Seventh Rhode Island remained at Falmouth until February 1863. Here Peckham again writes to Captain David R. Kenyon. He finally received his commission as second lieutenant; he learned that the responsibilities of an officer were greater than that of an enlisted man. In addition, many of the Seventh's officers had had enough with army life and had gone home.

*Camp of the 7th Regt R.I. Vols*
*Opposite Fredericksburg Jan 12, 1863*

*Capt D.R. Kenyon*
*Dear Friend*

*Yours of the eighth just came to hand last evening and with it came my Commission as 2nd Lieut. And your commission as Capt. is in my possession I do not know but as you are coming back? So soon as I will send it to you for it will make no difference in the amount of pay I presume, whether you accept it or not before you return. You are by general orders on Dress Parade this evening assigned to the command of company I Lieut Allen is made a first Lieut and assigned to Co. A[22] and I am with Lieut Daniels in Co. E[23] I do not like it very much but cannot help it the Cap tried to keep me but it was no use. I feel like a sheep in a pasture with dogs but never mind. it may all work our right eventually. Capt. Carr and Bennet[24], Lieut Inman, Brownell[25], and Haely[26] have resigned and gone home. Capt Leaven's,[27] Lieut Janks[28] and Hathaway[29] have got them on the course but dont you let any one know that I write you news for he had to incur his displeasure. I have one or two small tricks to inform you of but not by this. The boys do not feel any to well about his going home yet they are pleased with Lieut Allen. I am thinking some of trying to get out of this as soon as conveinient for I do not like the idea of crossing that river. And, now Capt. I am satisfied you do not like this war business any better then I do, and I know if I could get a furlough to R.I. I would never see the Army of the Potomac again soon, from various reasons and I never have expressed my belief that you would not come back but would resign and stay at home but some have thought it so and all say you are foolish to come back, I think from present indications there will be another move made soon toward Richmond and by way of Frederricksburg too Professor Lowe[30] in his Army gives us the intelligence that there are very few rebels in and around the city at this time but is sound and Jackson is tricky while Longstreet is plucky to resist us, as I think if we move at once we did, our Army will become demorilized quite as at Richmond here today that Burnside has proffered his resignation, it created some considerable rejoicing[31] in our camp for it was thought Little Mac,[32] would again be restored to his command and something effective be done, But I look for Hooker or Franklin[33] as his cucessor, and the "pop goes the wesel" for those of our officers who have not already resigned will make that a reason and off they will go for home. I do not blame them for I too will be with them probably, it will depend some upon circumstances, if I see a good chance of promotion I shall stay I am no 5 now on the roll of 2nd Lieutenants and there will be four more promotions within a few days and if Jenks resignation is accepted which it probably will it will give me another lift and I am anxiously waiting events as ever[34] I was and am no more sastified with 2nd Lt than I was Sergeant, now I want to be a 1st Lt More[35] is trying to get in Quartermaster, it can only be done by promoting Stanhope to the Captain, the officers all dislike Stanhope[36] very much we are getting along fine our mess and myself constitute it but we got the captains consent to let John Clarke be sutler[37] by his giving us half the profits he had given us at his retail prices what we ate since you left amounts to about a dollar a day, but when I come to mess with Lt. Daniels I expect it will cost me more for they are high livers but I am going to try to mess with You and live as cheap as I can and well we have not had my "flapjacks" since you left for we have nice warm baker bread[38] by enough to let through the day but good bye for this time hoping to here or see you soon. I am your Obt. Servant Peleg E. Peckham.*

Letter III. In 1864, President Abraham Lincoln did not believe that he would be reelected. If his opponent, George B. McClellan, were elected, he would negotiate peace with the Confederates and would thus permanently separate the United States of America. By the fall of 1864, the situation of war had changed, and the Federal forces finally appeared to be on the verge of victory. Lee was pinned at Petersburg, Phil Sheridan had cleared the Shenandoah Valley and William Tecumseh Sherman had captured Atlanta. To offset any further public sentiment, the *Providence Journal* published a series of soldiers' letters urging Rhode Islanders to vote for Lincoln, thus saving the Union. Major Peleg Peckham was one of them.

*Shannock Mills, RI Nov. 4, 1864*

*To the* Editor of the Journal:

*Next Tuesday is the day upon which is to be decided the nation's destiny.*

*The people are themselves by placing Abraham Lincoln or George B. McClellan in the Presidential chairs to decide whether by the election of Abraham Lincoln in shall "stand" the good old "Union" that it used to be, with its flag, the glorious old stars and stripes, in every port, over every town and hamlet, and over every fort from Maine to Mexico, with every vestige of the one great and only cause of this war wiped out and buried in the blood of patriots; so thoroughly removed and obliterated that no strife can ever grow out of its existence, "human slavery"; or wheter by the election of McClellan it shall "fall," be divided and subdivided into confederacies between which controversies, turmoil, and strife, resulting in war, will continually spring up and overthrow every possible foundation for an honorable peace. Shall we elect a man who is to proclaim an armistice and ask a negotiation with traitors and rebels with a view to compromise, and* this *at a time when the enemy is writhing and struggling in the last throes of armed resistance? I call upon every loyal citizen of Rhode Island, who has any interest in the welfare of his country, who has any sympathy with us who have fought for and carried and sustained our flag over more than two-thirds of the territory the enemy a short time since claimed as theirs, or who has the least particle of feeling and reverence for the memory of those who have been slain in this great war for human freedom and the maintenance of the best and most liberal government that every yet existed, to vote for Abraham Lincoln.*

*Suffer not yourselves, fellow citizens, to be deceived by the oily tongue of Jeff. Davis' emissaries, who I am sorry to state, in every town in our own New England, crying out* "Armistice and compromise alone will bring us an honorable peace.*" Now we all know what that* "honorable peace*" means, to them (Jeff Davis & Co.), simply the withdrawal of all our forces from every territory ever held by rebel authority; the raising of the blockade from all her ports, in short, the acknowledgement of the independence of the south, which will result in the final destruction of the government. This is what George B. McClellan if elected (which God forbid) promises on the Chicago platform to do for you. Bear this in mind as you go to the polls of Tuesday, and remember fellow citizen that your vote alone may turn the scale of the election in this State. So cast it for Abraham Lincoln and receive the last gratitude of Rhode Island's soldiers who are now fighting in the battles that will soon bring is* peace, and honorable peace.

*A Soldier*

# Lines on the Death

A common practice during the Civil War was to write a memorial poem in honor of a friend or relative who died in the conflict. The following poem was written in 1863 by Almon Knight in honor of his cousin, Alfred, who died of pneumonia at Falmouth, Virginia. Several stanzas were used as Alfred's epitaph.

*Lines on the Death of*
*Alfred S. Knight,*
*Private of Company C, 7th Regiment R.I.V.*
*Who died in the Regimental Hospital*
*Falmouth, January 31, 1863.*

*When last we saw him on his cheek,*
*The glow of health was bright,*
*The stamp of manhood on his brown,*
*And in his eye Hope's light.*

*He went from us with noble thoughts,*
*With high and holy aim,*
*With fond hope whispering in his heart,*
*That he'd come home again.*

*Alas! bright hope how vain*
*Are all thy flattering dreams!*
*How quickly pales the brightest star*
*That in thy future dreams!*

*Far from the home he loved so well*
*He met an early doom*
*No mother near to sooth his brow*
*Or cheer him mid deaths gloom.*

*No sister's gentle form was there*
*To hover round his bed,*
*To pillow with a sister's love*
*That wildly throbbing head.*

*Far from his kindred and from all*
*His fond heart held most dear,—*
*Oh! was there none in that far land*
*To shed for him a tear?*

*Was no one near in that sad hour,*
*That trembling hand to press;*
*To give for dear ones far away*
*Affection's last fond kiss?*

*Oh! yes; methinks, amongst that band*
*Of soldiers, brave and strong,*
*That many tears fell for him,*
*And that they'll mourn him long.*

*O Stricken parents weep no more*
*Bright the Crown to him that's given:*
*You'll meet your noble son again*
*In the bright land of heaven.*

*Brothers and sisters though he'll join*
*For here on Earth no more,*
*United you shall be again*
*On heavens immortal shore.*

# Appendix III

*No cruel Death can enter there,*
*In those bright realms above;*
*No parting tears are ever shed,*
*But all is peace and love.*

# Notes

## Appendix II

1. Stephen Farnum Peckham, *Peckham Genealogy: The English and American Descendents of John Peckham of Newport, Rhode Island* (New York, 1922), 404–5.
2. Hopkins, *The Seventh Regiment Rhode Island Volunteers in the Civil War, 1862–1865.* (Providence, RI: Snow and Farnum, 1903), 351.
3. *Narragansett Weekly*, December 27, 1862.
4. Edwin Stanton to Peleg E. Peckham, December 5, 1864, USAMHI.
5. William R.D. Blackwood to Albert S. Burdick, February 6, 1907, USAMHI; *Narragansett Weekly*, April 14, 1865.
6. Governor William Sprague of Rhode Island.
7. Colonel Zenas R. Bliss of Johnston commanded the Seventh. He commanded a brigade from 1863 until the summer of 1864 but did not become a general until 1892.
8. General James Nagle of Pennsylvania commanded the brigade to which the Seventh Rhode Island was attached.
9. General Samuel Sturgis commanded a division in the Ninth Corps and was later sent out west to fight Indians.
10. Captain Thomas B. Carr of Newport, Hopkins, *Seventh Regiment Rhode Island Volunteers*, 343–44.
11. First Lieutenant George B. Inman of Burrillville commanded the Ninth Corps ambulance train and was responsible for saving many of

the Seventh at Fredericksburg. He resigned shortly afterward. Hopkins, *Seventh Regiment Rhode Island Volunteers*, 361.

12. Second Lieutenant Charles T. Healey of Boston resigned right after Fredericksburg; *Revised Register of Rhode Island Volunteers*, vol. 1 (Providence, RI: E.L. Freeman, 1893), 407.

13. After Fredericksburg, Captain George Church became the Seventh's lieutenant colonel and was promoted to colonel of the Eleventh Rhode Island two months later, *Revised Register*, 354.

14. Captain Thomas Tobey of Smithfield was promoted to major in January 1863. He fell ill during the Mississippi Campaign and later joined the Regular Army, *Revised Register*, 419.

15. Second Lieutenant George Stone of Lawrence, Massachusetts, spent most of the Civil War in a variety of staff positions and ended it as a captain. Hopkins, *Seventh Regiment Rhode Island Volunteers*, 354–57.

16. The Twelfth Rhode Island was in the same brigade as the Seventh.

17. Private John D. Lewis of Hopkinton died of typhoid on December 25, 1862. He was buried at Wood River Cemetery, Richmond, Rhode Island, Hopkins, *Seventh Regiment Rhode Island Volunteers*, 437.

18. Private Joseph J. Kenyon of Company A died of typhoid at Falmouth, Virginia, on November 24, 1862, Hopkins, *Seventh Regiment Rhode Island Volunteers*, 437.

19. The Emancipation Proclamation.

20. Governor Horatio Seymour of New York was a war peace Democrat, also known as a "copperhead."

21. George B. McClellan was the first commander of the Army of the Potomac. He bungled the Peninsula and Maryland Campaigns and was removed from command in November 1862. Many soldiers resented the removal. He ran for president in 1864.

22. Edward R. Allen of South Kingstown. He eventually became a captain and accidentally shot himself in the foot at Petersburg. Company A came from southwestern Rhode Island, Hopkins, *Seventh Regiment Rhode Island Volunteers*, 338.

23. Lieutenant Percy Daniels of Woonsocket ended the war as lieutenant colonel, *Revised Register*, 359.

24. Captain Lyman A. Bennett of Warwick resigned on January 7, 1863, Hopkins, *Seventh Regiment Rhode Island Volunteers*, 340–43.

25. First Lieutenant Thomas S. Brownell of Newport resigned in January 1863, *Revised Register*, 348.

26. Charles T. Healey, a lieutenant in the Seventh.

27. Captain Lewis Leavens of Hopkinton commanded Company A and was wounded at Fredericksburg, Hopkins, *Seventh Regiment Rhode Island Volunteers*, 349–50.

28. Second Lieutenant Ethan Amos Jenks of Foster. He was wounded at Petersburg twice and ended the war as the Seventh's major, Hopkins, *Seventh Regiment Rhode Island Volunteers*, 346–47.

29. Second Lieutenant Cyrus B. Hathaway of Pawtucket, *Revised Register*, 374.

30. Thaddeus Lowe of New Hampshire was a volunteer who used balloons to spy on Confederate positions for the Army of the Potomac.

31. Peckham was one of the few men in the Seventh Rhode Island who was pleased that Ambrose Burnside had resigned; many Rhode Island soldiers were sympathetic to Burnside and felt that he had been let down by Washington.

32. George B. McClellan, the Army of the Potomac's first commander.

33. Joseph Hooker and William B. Franklin were two choices to replace Burnside; the command went to Hooker.

34. Officer's seniority was determined by the date of their commission. Jenks never resigned.

35. Lieutenant Winthrop A. Moore of East Greenwich ended the war as a captain, Hopkins, *Seventh Regiment Rhode Island Volunteers*, 350–51.

36. Quartermaster John R. Stanhope of Newport. He fell ill during the Mississippi Campaign and resigned in the fall of 1863, Hopkins, *Seventh Regiment Rhode Island Volunteers*, 330.

37. Unknown. The Seventh's sutler was William A. Gallagher of Warwick, Hopkins, *Seventh Regiment Rhode Island Volunteers*, 422–24.

38. Officers had to purchase their own food through government agents called sutlers.

# Further Reading

O ver the last 150 years, scores of books have been written about Rhode Island in the Civil War era. The following is not a comprehensive list, but it will allow the reader to seek more information about the state in the era. This is a list of the most readily available books, which can be found at the larger libraries in Rhode Island.

Allen George H. *Forty-six Months in the Fourth R.I. Volunteers.* Providence, RI: J.A. and R.A. Reid, Printers, 1887.

*An easy-to-read diary from an enlisted man who fought at New Berne and Antietam and at the Siege of Petersburg with the Fourth Rhode Island. A very good narrative on soldier life.*

Barker, Harold R. *History of Rhode Island Combat Units in the Civil War.* Providence: State of Rhode Island, 1964.

*Published during the Civil War centennial, this book is a good overview of Rhode Island in the period, as Barker summarizes each regimental history in an accessible text. This book is good for children.*

Bartlett, John R., ed. *Memoirs of Rhode Island Officers: Who Were Engaged in the Service of Their Country during the Great Rebellion with the South.* Providence, RI: Sydney S. Rider & Brothers Press, 1867.

*One of the best books about Rhode Island in the Civil War, this is a series of biographies about famous Rhode Island participants.*

Burrage, Henry S. *Brown University in the Civil War: A Memorial.* Providence, RI: Providence Press, 1868.

*A good study of Brown students who fought for the Union, with excellent biographical details.*

Chenery, William. *The Fourteenth Regiment Rhode Island Heavy Artillery in the War to Preserve the Union.* New York: Negro University Press, 1960.

*A history of Rhode Island's only black unit. Although heavily detailed on the lives of regimental officers, it does offer some good details on the role black troops played in the conflict.*

Denison, Frederic. *Sabres and Spurs: The First Rhode Island Cavalry in the Civil War.* Central Falls: First Rhode Island Cavalry Veterans Association, 1876.

*An excellent history of Rhode Island's only cavalry unit to serve in the eastern theater, this contains interesting aspects of combat and camp life.*

Grandchamp, Robert. *The Boys of Adams' Battery G: The Civil War through the Eyes of a Union Light Artillery Unit.* Jefferson, NC: McFarland, 2009.

*A modern study of a Rhode Island artillery battery. Highly recommended for those wanting a scholarly treatment of the Army of the Potomac's light artillery.*

Grandchamp, Robert. *The Seventh Rhode Island Infantry in the Civil War.* Jefferson, NC: McFarland, 2008.

*A heavily illustrated, modern update of the history of the Seventh Rhode Island.*

Grzyb, Frank. *Rhode Island's Civil War Hospital: Life and Death at Portsmouth Grove, 1861–1865.* Jefferson, NC: McFarland, 2012.

*A very readable, modern history of the large Civil War hospital located in Portsmouth.*

*Historical Sketch of Slocum Post, No. 10, Department of Rhode Island, Grand Army of the Republic.* Providence, RI: Snow and Farnum, 1892.

*A highly illustrated history of Rhode Island's largest Grand Army of the Republic Post.*

Hopkins, William P. *The Seventh Regiment Rhode Island Volunteers in the Civil War, 1862–1865.* Providence, RI: Snow and Farnum, 1903.

*Widely considered the best Rhode Island regimental history, it is well written in a diary format. It contains biographical information and hundreds of photographs.*

Jones, Daniel P. *The Economic and Social Transformation of Rural Rhode Island, 1780–1850.* Boston: Northeastern University Press, 1992.

*A must-read book on the social structure of western Rhode Island in the antebellum era.*

Rhodes, Elisha Hunt. *All for the Union: The Civil War Diary and Letters of Elisha Hunt Rhodes.* Edited by Robert Hunt Rhodes. Woonsocket, RI: Andrew Mobray, 1985.

*A classic diary that made Elisha Hunt Rhodes of the Second Rhode Island Volunteers one of the most famous "common soldiers" of the Civil War.*

Rhodes, John H. *History of Battery B, First Rhode Island Light Artillery.* Providence, RI: Snow and Farnum, 1894.

*One of the better Rhode Island battery histories. It is richly illustrated and contains an excellent narrative about Gettysburg and other battles in which the battery participated.*

VanDenBossche, Kris, ed. *Pleas Excuse All Bad Writing: A Documentary History of Rhode Island during the Civil War Era, 1861–1865*. Peace Dale, RI: Rhode Island Historical Document Transcription Project, 1993.

*Found at every public library in Rhode Island, this small text is a classic, containing transcribed diaries and letters from Rhode Island participants.*

Woodbury, Augustus. *A Narrative of the Campaign of the First Rhode Island Regiment in the Spring and Summer of 1861*. Providence, RI: Sydney S. Rider, 1862.

*Literally the first published regimental history, this small book set the standard for hundreds of others. This text is a good account of the hectic first days of Rhode Island's response to the conflict.*

In addition to this, manuscript material on Rhode Island in the Civil War era is readily available at the Rhode Island Historical Society, Rhode Island State Archives, Brown University, Newport Historical Society and the Westerly Library, among many others.

# Index

# About the Author

Robert Grandchamp was an eleventh-generation Rhode Islander and is now a first-generation Vermonter. He earned his MA in American history from Rhode Island College. Robert is the author of eight other books on American military history, including *The Seventh Rhode Island Infantry*, *Colonel Edward Cross*, *Providence to Fort Hell* and *The Boys of Adams' Battery G*, for which he was awarded the Order of Saint Barbara from the Rhode Island National Guard. In addition, he is a frequent book reviewer for *Blue & Gray* and *Civil War News*. A former National Park ranger, he is an analyst with the government and resides in Essex, Vermont.

ALSO BY ROBERT GRANDCHAMP

*Colonel Edward E. Cross: A Civil War Biography* (McFarland, 2012)
*Rhody Redlegs: The Providence Marine Corps of Artillery, 1801–2010* (McFarland, 2011)
*A Connecticut Yankee at War: The Life and Letters of Lt. George Lee Gaskell*
(Rhode Island College, 2010)
*The Boys of Adams' Battery G: The Civil War through the Eyes of a Union Light
Artillery Unit* (McFarland, 2009)
*The Seventh Rhode Island Infantry in the Civil War* (McFarland, 2008)
*Providence to Fort Hell: Letters from Company K, Seventh Rhode Island Volunteers*
(Heritage Books, 2007)
*With High and Holy Aim: Alfred Sheldon Knight and the Civil War*
(Publish America, 2006)
*With Their Usual Ardor: Scituate, Rhode Island and the American Revolution*
(Heritage Books, 2006)

Visit us at
www.historypress.net